PAST

E N T E R T A I N I N G

PASTA

ENTERTAINING

FABULOUS IDEAS FOR
SPECIAL OCCASION DISHES

Linda Fraser

HERMES
HOUSE

First published in 1998 by Hermes House

© Anness Publishing Limited 1998

Hermes House is an imprint ofAnness Publishing Limited
Hermes House, 88–89 Blackfriars Road, London SE1 8HA

ISBN 1 84038 191 4

A CIP catalogue record for this book is available from the British Library

Publisher: Joanna Lorenz
Senior Cookery Editor: Linda Fraser
Cookery Editors: Rosemary Wilkinson, Linda Doeser
Copy Editor: Val Barrett
Designers: Bill Mason, Siân Keogh
Illustrator: Anna Koska

Recipes: Catherine Atkinson, Carla Capalbo, Maxine Clark, Roz Denny, Christine France,
Sarah Gates, Shirley Gill, Norma MacMillan, Sue Maggs, Elizabeth Martin, Annie Nichols,
Jenny Stacy, Liz Trigg, Laura Washburn, Steven Wheeler
Photographs: Karl Adamson, Edward Allwright, David Armstrong, Steve Baxter, Jo Brewer,
James Duncan, Michelle Garrett, Amanda Heywood, Patrick McLeavey, Michael Michaels
Stylists: Madeleine Brehaut, Jo Brewer, Carla Capalbo, Michelle Garrett, Hilary Guy,
Amanda Heywood, Patrick McLeavey, Blake Minton, Kirsty Rawlings, Elizabeth Wolf-Cohen
Food for Photography: Wendy Lee, Lucy McKelvie, Jane Stevenson, Elizabeth Wolf-Cohen

Front Cover: Lisa Tai, Designer; Tom Odulate, Photographer;
Helen Trent, Stylist; Lucy McKelvie, Home Economist

Previously published as part of a larger compendium, *Best-Ever Pasta*

Printed in Hong Kong/China

1 3 5 7 9 10 8 6 4 2

NOTES
For all recipes, quantities are given in both metric and imperial measures and, where appropriate,
measures are also given in standard cups and spoons.
Follow one set, but not a mixture because they are not interchangeable.

Standard spoon and cup measurements are level.
1 tsp = 5ml, 1 tbsp = 15ml; 1 cup = 250ml/8fl oz

Australian standard tablespoons are 20ml. Australian readers should use 3 tsp in place of 1 tbsp for
measuring small quantities of gelatine, cornflour, salt, etc.

Medium eggs should be used unless otherwise stated.

CONTENTS

Introduction

Pasta is perfect for entertaining. Everybody loves it and most dishes can be prepared and cooked easily and quickly, allowing you to spend time with your guests, rather than isolated in the kitchen. There are dishes here for all tastes, from Italian classics, such as Tagliatelle with Prosciutto and Parmesan, to vegetarian specialities, such as Leek and Chèvre Lasagne.

The book begins with an introduction to the main types of pasta, a guide to useful sauces and pastes and step-by-step instructions for making fresh home-made pasta. The recipes are divided into six chapters: Soups, Fish & Seafood Dishes, Meat & Poultry Dishes, Vegetarian Dishes, Salads, and Desserts. The easy-to-follow-recipes are superbly illustrated in colour, and hints and tips throughout the book provide further information and suggestions.

Pasta is wonderfully versatile and goes well with almost all other ingredients, including meat, poultry, fish, seafood, vegetables, cheese and even fruit. It is highly nutritious, too, providing slow-burning energy, carbohydrate and protein. It is also economical, so you can invite friends to dinner more often.

The recipes in this book are mostly designed to serve four people, but quantities can easily be doubled or trebled for larger parties. A specific type of pasta is suggested in each recipe, but you can substitute your own favourites.

Pasta Types

When buying dried pasta, choose good-quality well-known brands. Of the "fresh" pasta sold in sealed packs in super-markets, the filled or stuffed varieties are worth buying; noodles and ribbon pasta are better bought dried, as these tend to have more bite when cooked. However, if you are lucky enough to live near an Italian delicatessen where pasta is made on the premises, it will usually be of very good quality. Fresh is not necessarily better, but the final choice is yours – the best pasta is home-made, as then you can be sure of the quality of the ingredients used and also of the finished texture.

You will see from this book that the sauces are almost limitless in their variety, as are the pasta shapes themselves. There are no hard-and-fast rules regarding which shape to use with which pasta sauce: it's really a matter of personal preference. However, there are a few guidelines to follow, such as that thin spaghetti suits seafood sauces, thicker spaghetti is good with creamy sauces and thick tubular pasta, like rigatoni, penne and so on, suits rustic sauces full of bits that will be caught in the pasta itself.

vermicelli

macaroni

quick-cook macaroni

fresh cuttlefish-ink tagliatelle

tagliatelle: tomato, spinach and plain

orzo or puntalette

small soup pasta

fresh caramellone

fresh ravioli

fresh cappellet[

fresh paglia e fieno ('straw and hay' tagliarini)

fresh tortellini

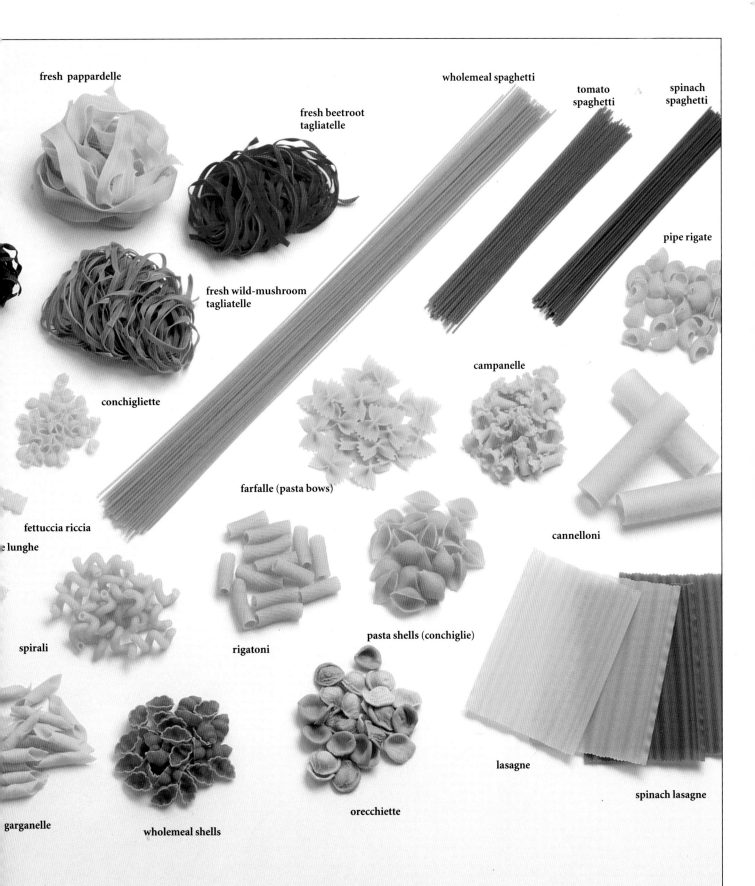

fresh pappardelle

fresh beetroot
tagliatelle

wholemeal spaghetti

tomato
spaghetti

spinach
spaghetti

fresh wild-mushroom
tagliatelle

pipe rigate

conchigliette

campanelle

farfalle (pasta bows)

cannelloni

fettuccia riccia
e lunghe

spirali

rigatoni

pasta shells (conchiglie)

lasagne

spinach lasagne

garganelle

wholemeal shells

orecchiette

Sauces and Pastes

There is an infinite variety of ready-made sauces and pastes available which you can add to your own sauce to make it richer or to deepen the flavour. Some can even be incorporated into pasta dough: for example, you can make mushroom or tomato or even pesto pasta.

Anchovies: salted Whole anchovies preserved in salt need to be rinsed and the backbone removed before use. They have a fresher flavour than canned anchovy fillets in oil. Used in moderation, anchovies add a fishy depth to sauces and soups.

Capers These are little green flower buds preserved in vinegar or salt. They add a sharp piquancy to rich sauces and are particularly good with tomatoes and many cheeses.

Carbonara sauce This is a delicious sauce made from cream, eggs, Parmesan and bacon or pancetta. Ready-made carbonara sauce is a useful standby for a quick meal – add sautéed fresh mushrooms or more bacon, if wished.

Garlic: chopped A great time-saver, eliminating the need for peeling and chopping. Use it straight out of the jar.

Mushroom paste A delicacy available from Italian delicatessens. Add a generous spoonful to freshly cooked pasta with a little cream for a quick sauce, or incorporate into dough to make delicious mushroom pasta.

Olive paste Cuts out all that stoning and chopping. Delicious stirred into hot pasta with chopped fresh tomato or added by the spoonful to enrich a tomato or meat sauce.

Pesto The commercial version of fresh basil pesto. Brands vary, but it is a very useful store-cupboard standby to stir into hot pasta and soups.

Pesto: fresh Some supermarkets produce their own "fresh" pesto, sold in tubs in the chilled cabinet. This is infinitely superior to the bottled variety, although your own freshly made pesto will be even better.

Pesto: red A commercial sauce made from tomatoes and red peppers to stir into hot pasta or to pep up soups.

Tomato pasta sauce Again, a good standby or base for a quick meal. Vary by adding chopped anchovies and olives, or pour over freshly cooked stuffed pasta such as tortellini.

Tomato purée An essential if you are making a sauce from insipid fresh tomatoes. It will intensify any tomato-based sauce and will help thicken meat sauces. It will also make tomato pasta if added to the basic dough ingredients.

Tomatoes: canned plum No store-cupboard should be without these – invaluable for making any tomato sauce or stew when good fresh tomatoes are not readily available.

Tomatoes: canned chopped Usually made from Italian plum tomatoes which have a fuller flavour than most, these are the heart of a good tomato sauce if you cannot find really ripe, red, tasty, fresh tomatoes.

Tomatoes: passata A useful store-cupboard ingredient, this is pulped tomato that has been strained to remove the seeds. It makes a good base for a tomato sauce, though chopped canned tomatoes can also be used.

Tomatoes: sun-dried in oil These tomatoes are drained and chopped and added to tomato-based dishes to give a deeper, almost roasted tomato flavour.

Below, clockwise from top left: Salted anchovies; canned chopped tomatoes; pesto; olive paste; canned plum tomatoes; tomato purée; passata.

Eastern Pasta

Various forms of noodle or pasta exist outside Europe and America. They are found mainly in China and Japan, but also throughout Malaysia, Hong Kong and the rest of the Far East, including parts of India and Tibet.

This pasta, usually in noodle form and often enhanced with a sprinkling of vegetables or fish, adds variety to the sometimes monotonous staple diet of rice and beans eaten by the poorer sections of the population. Some types of pasta are used to give bulk to soups; others are eaten as a filling dish to stave off hunger during the day. They are made from the staple crops of each region – whether rice flour, soya bean flour or potato flour – and are cooked in different ways: some are soaked and then fried, some are boiled and fried and some are rolled out and stuffed like ravioli, but most are simply boiled. Some turn transparent when cooked.

Oriental egg noodles are usually made with wheat flour and can be treated in the same way as ordinary Western pasta. Buckwheat and fresh wholemeal noodles are cooked in a similar fashion. Fresh white noodles do not contain egg but are cooked in the same way as egg noodles. Some dried egg noodles come in discs or blocks and are "cooked" by immersion in boiling water in which they are then left to soak for a few minutes. As with Western pasta, oriental noodles can be flavoured with additional

ingredients such as prawns, carrot and spinach.

Won ton skins, like thin squares of rolled-out pasta, are used for stuffing and making different filled shapes. Although oriental pasta is available in a variety of long noodle types, it doesn't seem to be made into the shapes we are used to seeing in Europe and America: you will often find it wound into balls and beautifully packaged.

Above: Eastern noodles include (from top left, clockwise) oriental rice flour noodles, rice vermicelli, rice stick noodles, handmade amoy flour vermicelli, medium egg noodles, fresh brown mein, egg noodles, rice stick vermicelli, fresh thin egg noodles, Japanese wheat flour noodles, Ho Fan vermicelli, spinach vegetable noodles, carrot vegetable noodles, won ton skins, wheat flour noodles, fresh white mein, buckwheat noodles, shrimp egg noodles.

About Pasta

Most pasta is made from durum wheat flour and water – durum is a special kind of wheat with a very high protein content. Egg pasta, *pasta all'uova*, contains flour and eggs, and is used for flat pasta such as tagliatelle, or for lasagne. Very little wholemeal pasta is eaten in Italy, but it is quite popular in other countries.

All these types of pasta are available dried in packets and will keep almost indefinitely. Fresh pasta is now widely available and can be bought in most good supermarkets. It can be very good, but can never compare to home-made egg pasta.

Pasta comes in countless shapes and sizes. It is very difficult to give a definitive list, as the names for the shapes vary from country to country. In some cases, just within Italy, the same shape can appear with several different names, depending upon which region it is in. The pasta shapes called for in this book, as well as many others, are illustrated in the introduction. The most common names have been listed there.

Most of the recipes in this book specify the pasta shape most appropriate for a particular sauce. They can, of course, be replaced with another kind. A general rule is that long pasta goes better with tomato or thinner sauces, while short pasta is best for chunkier, meatier sauces. But this rule should not be followed too rigidly. Part of the fun of cooking and eating pasta is in the endless possible combinations of sauce and pasta shapes.

How to Make Egg Pasta by Hand

This classic recipe for egg pasta from Emilia Romagna region, around Bolognia, calls for just three ingredients; flour, eggs and a little salt. In other regions of Italy water, milk or oil are sometimes added. Use plain or strong white flour, and large eggs. As a general guide, use 50g/2oz/½ cup of flour to each egg. Quantities will vary with the exact size of the eggs.

To serve 3–4
150g/5oz/1¼ cups flour
2 eggs
pinch of salt

To serve 4–6
210g/7½oz/scant 2
    cups flour
3 eggs
pinch of salt

To serve 6–8
275g/10oz/2½ cups flour
4 eggs
pinch of salt

1 Place the flour in the centre of a clean, smooth work surface. Make a well in the middle. Break the eggs into the well. Add a pinch of salt.

2 Start beating the eggs with a fork, gradually drawing the flour from the inside walls of the well. As the pasta thickens, continue the mixing with your hands. Incorporate as much flour as possible until the mixture forms a mass. It will still be lumpy. If it still sticks to your hands, add a little more flour. Set the dough aside. Scrape off all traces of the dough from the work surface until it is perfectly smooth. Wash and dry your hands.

3 Lightly flour the work surface. Knead the dough by pressing it away from you with the heel of your hands, and then folding it over towards you. Repeat this action over and over, turning the dough as you knead. Work for about 10 minutes, or until the dough is smooth and elastic.

4 If you are using more than two eggs, divide the dough in half. Flour the rolling pin and the work surface. Pat the dough into a disc and begin rolling it out into a flat circle, rotating it a quarter turn after each roll to keep its shape round. Roll until the disc is about 3mm/⅛in thick.

time to keep it evenly thin. By the end (this process should not last more than 8 to 10 minutes or the dough will lose its elasticity) the whole sheet should be smooth and almost transparent. If the dough is still sticky, lightly flour your hands as you continue rolling and stretching it in the same way.

8 To cut tagliatelle, fettuccine or tagliolini, fold the sheet of pasta into a flat roll about 10cm/4in wide. Cut across the roll to form noodles of the desired width. Tagliolini is 3mm/⅛in; fettuccine is 4mm/⅙in; tagliatelle is 5mm/¼in. After cutting, open out the noodles and let them dry for about 5 minutes before cooking. These noodles may be stored for some weeks without refrigeration. Allow the noodles to dry completely before storing them, uncovered, in a dry cupboard, and use as required.

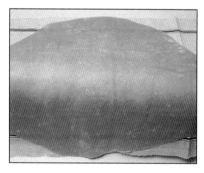

5 Roll out the dough until it is paper-thin by rolling up on to the rolling pin and simultaneously giving a sideways stretch with your hands. Wrap the near edge of the dough around the centre of the rolling pin and begin rolling the dough up away from you. As you roll back and forth, slide your hands from the centre towards the outer edges of the pin, stretching and thinning out the pasta.

6 Quickly repeat these movements until about two-thirds of the sheet of pasta is wrapped around the pin. Lift and turn the wrapped pasta sheet about 45° before unrolling it. Repeat the rolling and stretch process, starting from a new point of the sheet each

7 If you are making pasta noodles, such as tagliatelle, fettuccine, etc, lay a clean dish towel on a table or other flat surface, and unroll the pasta sheet onto it, letting about one-third of the sheet hang over the edge of the table. Rotate the dough about every 10 minutes. Roll out the second sheet of dough if you are using more than two eggs. After 25–30 minutes the pasta will have dried enough to cut. Do not allow to overdry or the pasta will crack as it is cut.

9 To cut the pasta for lasagne or pappardelle, do not fold or dry the rolled-out dough. Lasagne is made from rectangles approximately 13 × 9cm/5 × 3½in. Pappardelle are large noodles cut with a fluted pasta or pastry wheel. They are about 2cm/¾in wide.

SOUPS

~

Provençal Fish Soup with Pasta

This colourful soup has all the flavours of the Mediterranean. Serve it as a main course for a deliciously filling lunch.

Serves 4

30ml/2 tbsp olive oil

1 onion, sliced

1 garlic clove, crushed

1 leek, sliced

225g/8oz canned chopped tomatoes

pinch of Mediterranean herbs

1.5ml/¼ tsp saffron strands (optional)

115g/4oz small pasta

about 8 live mussels in the shell

450g/1lb filleted and skinned white fish, such as cod, plaice or monkfish

salt and ground black pepper

For the rouille

2 garlic cloves, crushed

1 canned pimiento, drained and chopped

15ml/1 tbsp fresh white breadcrumbs

60ml/4 tbsp mayonnaise

toasted French bread, to serve

1 Heat the oil in a large saucepan and add the onion, garlic and leek. Cover and cook gently for 5 minutes, stirring occasionally until the vegetables are soft.

2 Pour in 1 litre/1¾pints/4 cups water, the tomatoes, herbs, saffron and pasta. Season with salt and ground black pepper and cook for 15–20 minutes.

3 Scrub the mussels and pull off the "beards". Discard any that will not close when sharply tapped.

4 Cut the fish into bite-size chunks and add to the soup, placing the mussels on top. Then simmer with the lid on for 5-10 minutes until the mussels open and the fish is just cooked. Discard any unopened mussels.

5 To make the rouille, pound the garlic, canned pimiento and breadcrumbs together in a pestle and mortar (or in a blender or food processor). Stir in the mayonnaise and season well.

6 Spread the toasted French bread with the rouille and serve with the soup.

Pasta, Bean and Vegetable Soup

This colourful, filling soup will satisfy the largest appetite.

INGREDIENTS

Serves 4–6

115g/4oz dried borlotti or black-eyed beans, soaked overnight and drained

1.2 litres/2 pints/5 cups vegetable, poultry or meat stock

1 large onion, chopped

1 large garlic clove, finely chopped

2 celery sticks, chopped

½ red pepper, seeded and chopped

350g/12oz tomatoes, skinned, seeded and chopped or canned chopped tomatoes

225g/8oz smoked bacon loin

75g/3oz tiny soup pasta

2 courgettes, halved lengthways and sliced

15ml/1 tbsp tomato purée

salt and ground black pepper

shredded fresh basil, to garnish

1 Put the beans in a large pan. Cover with fresh cold water and bring to the boil. Boil for 10 minutes, then drain and rinse. Return the beans to the pan, add the stock and bring to the boil. Skim off the scum.

2 Add the onion, garlic, celery, red pepper, tomatoes and bacon. Bring back to the boil.

3 Cover and simmer over a low heat for 1½ hours or until the beans are just tender. Lift out the bacon. Shred the meat coarsely with two forks and set aside.

4 Add the pasta, courgettes and tomato purée to the soup. Season to taste with salt and pepper. Simmer uncovered, for a further 5–8 minutes, stirring the soup occasionally. (Check the pasta cooking time on the packet.)

5 Stir in the shredded bacon. Taste and adjust the seasoning if necessary, then serve the soup hot, sprinkled with shredded fresh basil as a garnish.

Courgette Soup with Small Pasta Shells

A pretty, fresh-tasting soup which could be made using cucumber instead of courgettes.

INGREDIENTS

Serves 4–6

60ml/4 tbsp olive or sunflower oil

2 onions, finely chopped

1.5 litres/2½ pints/6¼ cups chicken stock

900g/2lb courgettes

115g/4oz small soup pasta

freshly squeezed lemon juice

30ml/2 tbsp chopped fresh chervil

salt and ground black pepper

soured cream, to serve

1 Heat the oil in a large saucepan and add the onions. Cover and cook gently for about 20 minutes until very soft but not coloured, stirring occasionally.

2 Add the chicken stock to the saucepan and bring the mixture to the boil.

3 Meanwhile grate the courgettes and stir into the boiling stock with the pasta. Reduce the heat and simmer for 15 minutes until the pasta is tender. Season to taste with lemon juice, salt and pepper.

4 Stir in the chopped fresh chervil and add a swirl of soured cream before serving.

Chunky Pasta Soup

Serve this filling main-meal soup with tasty, pesto-topped French bread croûtons.

INGREDIENTS

Serves 4

115g/4oz/⅔ cup dry beans (a mixture of
   red kidney and haricot beans), soaked
   in cold water overnight
15ml/1 tbsp oil
1 onion, chopped
2 celery sticks, thinly sliced
2–3 garlic cloves, crushed
2 leeks, thinly sliced
1 vegetable stock cube
400g/14oz can or jar of pimientos
45–60ml/3–4 tbsp tomato purée
115g/4oz pasta shapes
4 pieces French bread
15ml/1 tbsp pesto sauce
115g/4oz/1 cup baby sweetcorn, halved
50g/2oz each broccoli and
   cauliflower florets
few drops of Tabasco sauce, to taste
salt and ground black pepper

1 Drain the beans and place in a large saucepan with 1.2 litres/ 2 pints/5 cups water. Bring to the boil and simmer for about 1 hour, or until nearly tender.

2 When the beans are almost ready, heat the oil in a large pan and fry the vegetables for 2 minutes. Add the stock cube and the beans with 600ml/1 pint/ 2 cups of their liquid. Cover and simmer for 10 minutes.

3 Meanwhile, purée the pimientos with a little of their liquid and add to the pan. Stir in the tomato purée and pasta and cook for 15 minutes. Preheat the oven to 200°C/400°F/Gas 6.

4 Meanwhile, make the pesto croûtons; spread the French bread with the pesto sauce and bake for 10 minutes, or until crispy.

5 When the pasta is just cooked, add the sweetcorn, broccoli and cauliflower florets, Tabasco sauce and seasoning to taste. Heat through for 2–3 minutes and serve at once with the croûtons.

Red Onion and Beetroot Soup

This beautiful, vivid ruby-red soup will look stunning at any dinner-party table.

INGREDIENTS

Serves 4–6

15ml/1 tbsp olive oil

350g/12oz red onions, sliced

2 garlic cloves, crushed

275g/10oz cooked beetroot, cut into sticks

1.2 litres/2 pints/5 cups vegetable stock
   or water

50g/2oz cooked soup pasta

30ml/2 tbsp raspberry vinegar

salt and ground black pepper

low-fat yogurt or fromage blanc,
   to garnish

snipped chives, to garnish

3 Add the beetroot, stock or water, cooked soup pasta and vinegar, and heat through. Season to taste with salt and pepper.

4 Ladle into warmed soup bowls. Top each one with a spoonful of low-fat yogurt or fromage blanc and sprinkle with chives.

1 Heat the olive oil in a flame-proof casserole and add the onions and garlic.

2 Cook gently for 20 minutes or until the onions and garlic are soft and tender.

Thai Chicken Soup

This classic Oriental soup now enjoys worldwide popularity.

INGREDIENTS

Serves 4

15ml/1 tbsp vegetable oil

1 garlic clove, finely chopped

2 boneless chicken breasts, about
175g/6oz each, skinned and chopped

2.5ml/½ tsp ground turmeric

1.5ml/¼ tsp hot chilli powder

75g/3oz creamed coconut

900ml/1½ pints/3¾ cups hot
chicken stock

30ml/2 tbsp lemon or lime juice

30ml/2 tbsp crunchy peanut butter

50g/2oz thread egg noodles, broken into
small pieces

15ml/1 tbsp spring onions, finely chopped

15ml/1 tbsp chopped fresh coriander

salt and ground black pepper

30ml/2 tbsp desiccated coconut and
½ fresh red chilli, seeded and finely
chopped, to garnish

1 Heat the oil in a large pan and fry the garlic for 1 minute until lightly golden. Add the chicken and spices and stir-fry for a further 3–4 minutes.

2 Crumble the creamed coconut into the hot chicken stock and stir until dissolved. Pour on to the chicken then add the lemon or lime juice, peanut butter and egg noodles.

3 Cover and simmer for about 15 minutes. Add the spring onions and fresh coriander, then season well and cook for a further 5 minutes.

4 Meanwhile, place the desiccated coconut and chilli in a small frying pan and heat for 2–3 minutes, stirring frequently, until the coconut is lightly browned.

5 Serve the soup in warmed bowls sprinkled with the fried coconut and chilli.

Parmesan and Cauliflower Soup

*A silky smooth, mildly cheesy soup
which isn't overpowered by the
cauliflower. It makes an elegant
dinner-party soup served with crisp
Melba toast.*

INGREDIENTS

Serves 6

1 large cauliflower

1.2 litres/2 pints/5 cups chicken or
    vegetable stock

175g/6oz farfalle

150ml/¼ pint/⅔ cup single cream or milk

freshly grated nutmeg

pinch of cayenne pepper

60ml/4 tbsp freshly grated
    Parmesan cheese

salt and ground black pepper

For the Melba toast

3–4 slices day-old white bread

freshly grated Parmesan cheese,
    for sprinkling

1.5ml/¼ tsp paprika

1 Cut the leaves and central stalk
away from the cauliflower and
discard. Divide the cauliflower into
similar-size florets.

2 Bring the stock to the boil and
add the cauliflower. Simmer
for about 10 minutes or until very
soft. Remove the cauliflower with a
slotted spoon and place in a
blender or food processor.

3 Add the pasta to the stock and
simmer for 10 minutes until
tender. Drain, reserve the pasta,
and pour the liquid over the cauliflower. Add the cream or milk,
nutmeg and cayenne to the cauliflower. Blend until smooth, then

press through a sieve. Stir in the
cooked pasta. Reheat the soup and
stir in the Parmesan. Taste and
adjust the seasoning if necessary.

4 Meanwhile make the Melba
toast. Preheat the oven to
180°C/350°F/Gas 4. Toast the
bread lightly on both sides.
Quickly cut off the crusts and split
each slice in half horizontally.
Scrape off any doughy bits and
sprinkle with Parmesan and
paprika. Place on a baking sheet
and bake in the oven for about
10–15 minutes or until uniformly
golden. Serve with the soup.

Minestrone

A substantial and popular winter soup originally from Milan, but found in various versions around the Mediterranean coasts of Italy and France. Cut the vegetables as roughly or as small as you like. Add freshly grated Parmesan cheese just before serving.

INGREDIENTS

Serves 6–8

225g/8oz/2 cups dried haricot beans
30ml/2 tbsp olive oil
50g/2oz smoked streaky bacon, diced
2 large onions, sliced
2 garlic cloves, crushed
2 carrots, diced
3 celery sticks, sliced
400g/14oz canned chopped tomatoes
2.25 litres/4 pints/10 cups beef stock
350g/12oz potatoes, diced
175g/6oz small pasta shapes, such as
    macaroni, stars, shells, etc
225g/8oz green cabbage, thinly sliced
175g/6oz fine green beans, sliced
115g/4oz/1 cup frozen peas
45ml/3 tbsp chopped fresh parsley
salt and ground black pepper
freshly grated Parmesan cheese, to serve

1 Cover the beans with cold water in a bowl and leave to soak overnight.

2 Heat the oil in a large saucepan and add the bacon, onions and garlic. Cover and cook gently for 5 minutes, stirring occasionally.

3 Add the carrots and celery and cook for 2–3 minutes until the vegetables are softening.

4 Drain the beans and add to the pan with the tomatoes and the beef stock. Cover and simmer for 2–2½ hours, until the beans are tender.

5 Add the potatoes 30 minutes before the soup is ready.

6 Add the pasta, cabbage, beans, peas and parsley 15 minutes before the soup is ready. Season to taste and serve with a bowl of freshly grated Parmesan cheese.

Consommé with Agnolotti

A delicious and satisfying consommé with wonderful flavours.

INGREDIENTS

Serves 4–6

75g/3oz cooked peeled prawns

75g/3oz canned crab meat, drained

5ml/1 tsp fresh root ginger, peeled and finely grated

15ml/1 tbsp fresh white breadcrumbs

5ml/1 tsp light soy sauce

1 spring onion, finely chopped

1 garlic clove, crushed

1 quantity of basic pasta dough

flour, for dusting

egg white, beaten

400g/14oz can chicken or fish consommé

30ml/2 tbsp sherry or vermouth

salt and ground black pepper

50g/2oz cooked, peeled prawns and fresh coriander leaves, to garnish

1 To make the filling, put the prawns, crab meat, ginger, breadcrumbs, soy sauce, onion, garlic and seasoning into a food processor or blender and process until smooth.

2 Roll the pasta into thin sheets and dust lightly with flour. Stamp out 32 rounds 5cm/2in in diameter, with a fluted pastry cutter.

3 Place a small teaspoon of the filling in the centre of half the pasta rounds. Brush the edges of each round with egg white and sandwich together with a second round on top. Pinch the edges together firmly to stop the filling seeping out.

4 Cook the pasta in a large pan of boiling salted water for 5 minutes (cook in batches to stop them sticking together). Remove and drop into a bowl of cold water for 5 seconds before placing on a tray. (You can make these pasta shapes a day in advance. Cover with clear film and store in the fridge until required.)

5 Heat the chicken or fish consommé in a pan with the sherry or vermouth. When piping hot, add the pasta shapes and simmer for 1–2 minutes.

6 Serve in a shallow soup bowl covered with hot consommé. Garnish with extra peeled prawns and fresh coriander leaves.

FISH &
SEAFOOD
DISHES

~

Tuna Lasagne

Serves 6

1 quantity fresh pasta dough, cut for
    lasagne, or 375g/12oz no-precook
    dried lasagne
15g/½oz butter
1 small onion, finely chopped
1 garlic clove, finely chopped
115g/4oz mushrooms, thinly sliced
60ml/4 tbsp dry white wine (optional)
600ml/1 pint/2½ cups white sauce
150ml/¼ pint/⅔ cup whipping cream
45ml/3 tbsp chopped parsley
2 x 200g/7oz cans tuna, drained
2 canned pimientos, cut into strips
65g/2½oz/generous ½ cup frozen
    peas, thawed
115g/4oz mozzarella cheese, grated
30ml/2 tbsp freshly grated
    Parmesan cheese
salt and ground black pepper

1 For fresh lasagne, bring a large pan of salted water to the boil. Cook the lasagne, in small batches, until almost tender to the bite. For dried lasagne, soak in a bowl of hot water for 3–5 minutes.

2 Place the lasagne in a colander and rinse with cold water. Lay on a dish towel to drain.

3 Preheat the oven to 180°C/ 350°F//Gas 4. Melt the butter in a saucepan and cook the onion until soft.

4 Add the garlic and mushrooms, and cook until soft, stirring occasionally. Pour in the wine, if using. Boil for 1 minute. Add the white sauce, cream and parsley. Season.

5 Spoon a thin layer of sauce over the base of a 30 × 23cm/ 12 × 9in baking dish. Cover with a layer of lasagne sheets.

6 Flake the tuna. Scatter half the tuna, pimiento strips, peas and mozzarella over the lasagne. Spoon one-third of the remaining sauce over the top, cover with another layer of lasagne sheets.

7 Repeat the layers, ending with pasta and sauce. Sprinkle with the Parmesan. Bake for 30–40 minutes or until lightly browned.

Pasta Bows with Smoked Salmon and Dill

In Italy, pasta cooked with smoked salmon is very fashionable. This is a quick and luxurious sauce.

INGREDIENTS

Serves 4

6 spring onions
50g/2oz/4 tbsp butter
90ml/6 tbsp dry white wine or vermouth
450ml/¾ pint/1¾ cups double cream
freshly grated nutmeg
225g/8oz smoked salmon
30ml/2 tbsp chopped fresh dill or
    15ml/1 tbsp dried
freshly squeezed lemon juice
450g/1lb farfalle
salt and ground black pepper

1 Slice the spring onions finely. Melt the butter in a saucepan and gently fry the spring onions for 1 minute until softened.

2 Add the wine or vermouth and boil hard to reduce to about 30ml/2 tbsp. Stir in the cream and add salt, pepper and nutmeg to taste. Bring to the boil and simmer for 2–3 minutes until the sauce is slightly thickened.

3 Cut the smoked salmon into 2.5cm/1in squares and stir into the sauce with the dill. Taste and add a little lemon juice. Keep the sauce warm.

4 Cook the pasta in plenty of boiling salted water according to the instructions on the packet. Drain well. Toss the pasta with the sauce and serve immediately.

Spaghetti with Hot-and-sour Fish

*A truly Chinese spicy taste is what
makes this sauce so different.*

INGREDIENTS

Serves 4

350g/12oz spaghetti

450g/1lb monkfish, skinned

225g/8oz courgettes

1 green chilli, cored and seeded (optional)

15ml/1 tbsp olive oil

1 large onion, chopped

5ml/1 tsp turmeric

115g/4oz/1 cup shelled peas, thawed
   if frozen

10ml/2 tsp lemon juice

75ml/5 tbsp hoisin sauce

150ml/¼ pint/⅔ cup water

salt and ground black pepper

fresh dill sprig, to garnish

1 Cook the pasta in plenty of
boiling salted water according
to the instructions on the packet.

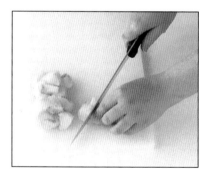

2 Cut the monkfish into bite-size
pieces. Thinly slice the
courgettes, then finely chop the
chilli, if using.

3 Heat the oil in a large frying
pan and fry the onion for
5 minutes until softened. Add
the turmeric.

4 Add the chilli, if using,
courgettes and peas, and fry
over a medium heat for 5 minutes
until the vegetables have softened.

5 Stir in the fish, lemon juice,
hoisin sauce and water. Bring
to the boil, then simmer,
uncovered, for about 5 minutes or
until the fish is tender. Season.

6 Drain the pasta thoroughly and
turn into a serving dish. Toss in
the sauce to coat. Serve at once,
garnished with fresh dill.

Smoked Trout Cannelloni

Smoked trout can be bought already filleted or whole. If you buy fillets, you'll need 225g/8oz.

INGREDIENTS

Serves 4–6

1 large onion, finely chopped

1 garlic clove, crushed

60ml/4 tbsp vegetable stock

2 x 400g/14oz cans chopped tomatoes

2.5ml/½ tsp dried mixed herbs

1 smoked trout, about 400g/14oz

75g/3oz/¾ cup frozen peas, thawed

75g/3oz/1½ cups fresh breadcrumbs

16 cannelloni tubes

salt and ground black pepper

mixed salad, to serve (optional)

25ml/1½ tbsp freshly grated
  Parmesan cheese

For the cheese sauce

25g/1oz/2 tbsp margarine

25g/1oz/¼ cup plain flour

350ml/12fl oz/1½ cups skimmed milk

freshly grated nutmeg

1 Simmer the onion, garlic and stock in a large covered saucepan for 3 minutes. Uncover and continue to cook, stirring occasionally, until the stock has reduced entirely.

2 Stir in the tomatoes and dried herbs. Simmer, uncovered, for a further 10 minutes, or until the mixture is very thick.

3 Meanwhile, skin the smoked trout with a sharp knife. Carefully flake the flesh and discard the bones. Mix the fish together with the tomato mixture, peas, breadcrumbs, salt and ground black pepper.

4 Preheat the oven to 190°C/ 375°F/Gas 5. Spoon the filling into the cannelloni tubes and arrange in an ovenproof dish.

5 For the sauce, put the margarine, flour and milk into a saucepan and cook over a medium heat, whisking constantly until the sauce thickens. Simmer for 2–3 minutes, stirring all the time. Season to taste with salt, pepper and nutmeg.

6 Pour the sauce over the cannelloni and sprinkle with the grated Parmesan cheese. Bake in the oven for 35–40 minutes, or until the top is golden and bubbling. Serve with a mixed salad, if desired.

Stir-fried Noodles with Sweet Salmon

A delicious sauce forms the marinade for the salmon in this recipe. Served with soft-fried noodles, it makes a stunning dish.

INGREDIENTS

Serves 4

350g/12oz salmon fillet

30ml/2 tbsp Japanese soy sauce (shoyu)

30ml/2 tbsp sake

60ml/4 tbsp mirin or sweet sherry

5ml/1 tsp light brown soft sugar

10ml/2 tsp grated fresh root ginger

3 cloves garlic, 1 crushed, and 2 sliced into
   rounds

30ml/2 tbsp groundnut oil

225g/8oz dried egg noodles, cooked
   and drained

50g/2oz alfalfa sprouts

30ml/2 tbsp sesame seeds, lightly toasted

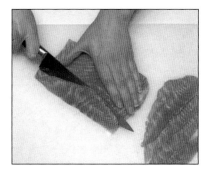

1 Thinly slice the salmon, then place in a shallow dish.

2 In a bowl, mix together the soy sauce, sake, mirin or sherry, sugar, ginger and crushed garlic. Pour over the salmon, cover and leave to marinate for 30 minutes.

3 Drain the salmon, scraping off and reserving the marinade. Place the salmon in a single layer on a baking sheet. Cook under a preheated grill for 2–3 minutes, without turning.

4 Meanwhile, heat a wok until hot, add the oil and swirl it around. Add the garlic rounds and cook until golden brown, but do not allow them to burn.

5 Add the cooked noodles and reserved marinade to the wok. Stir-fry for 3–4 minutes, until the marinade has reduced slightly to make a syrupy glaze that coats the egg noodles.

6 Toss in the alfalfa sprouts, then remove immediately from the heat. Transfer to warmed serving plates and top with the salmon. Sprinkle over the toasted sesame seeds. Serve at once.

COOK'S TIP

It is important to scrape the marinade off the fish as any remaining pieces of ginger or garlic would burn during grilling and spoil the finished dish.

Pasta with Tuna, Capers and Anchovies

This piquant sauce could be made without the addition of tomatoes – just heat the oil, add the other ingredients and heat through gently before tossing with the pasta.

Serves 4

400g/14oz can tuna fish in oil
30ml/2 tbsp olive oil
2 garlic cloves, crushed
800g/1¾lb canned chopped tomatoes
6 canned anchovy fillets, drained
30ml/2 tbsp capers in vinegar, drained
30ml/2 tbsp chopped fresh basil
450g/1lb rigatoni, penne or garganelle
salt and ground black pepper
fresh basil sprigs, to garnish

1 Drain the oil from the can of tuna fish into a large saucepan, add the olive oil and heat gently until the oil mixture stops spitting.

2 Add the garlic and fry until golden. Stir in the tomatoes and simmer for about 25 minutes until thickened.

3 Flake the tuna and cut the anchovies in half. Stir into the sauce with the capers and chopped basil. Season well.

4 Cook the pasta in plenty of boiling salted water according to the instructions on the packet. Drain well and toss with the sauce. Garnish with fresh basil sprigs.

Smoked Haddock and Pasta in Parsley Sauce

A creamy and delicious pasta dish with a crunchy almond topping.

INGREDIENTS

Serves 4

450g/1lb smoked haddock fillet

1 small leek or onion, sliced thickly

300ml/½ pint/1¼ cups milk

1 bouquet garni (bay leaf, thyme and
  parsley stalks)

25g/1oz margarine

25g/1oz plain flour

225g/8oz pasta shells

30ml/2 tbsp chopped fresh parsley

salt and freshly ground black pepper

15g/½oz toasted flaked almonds,
  to garnish

3 Put the margarine, flour and reserved milk into a pan. Bring to the boil and whisk constantly until smooth. Season, then add the fish and leek or onion.

4 Cook the pasta in a large pan of boiling water until tender, but still firm to the bite. Drain and stir into the sauce with the chopped parsley. Serve at once, scattered with almonds.

1 Remove all the skin and any bones from the haddock. Put into a pan with the leek or onion, milk and bouquet garni. Bring to the boil, cover and simmer gently for about 8–10 minutes, until the fish flakes easily.

2 Strain, reserving the milk for making the sauce, and discard the bouquet garni.

Baked Seafood Spaghetti

In this dish, each portion is baked and served in an individual packet which is then opened at the table. Use baking parchment paper or foil to make the packets.

INGREDIENTS

Serves 4

450g/1lb fresh mussels

120ml/4fl oz/½ cup dry white wine

60ml/4 tbsp olive oil

2 garlic cloves, finely chopped

450g/1lb tomatoes, fresh or canned, peeled and finely chopped

400g/14oz spaghetti or other long pasta

225g/8oz/2 cups peeled and deveined prawns, fresh or frozen

30ml/2 tbsp chopped fresh parsley

salt and ground black pepper

1 Scrub the mussels well under cold running water, cutting off the "beards" with a small sharp knife. Discard any that do not close when tapped sharply. Place the mussels and the wine in a large saucepan and heat until opened.

2 Lift out the mussels and remove to a side dish. Discard any that do not open. Strain the cooking liquid into a bowl through kitchen paper and reserve until needed. Preheat the oven to 150°C/300°F/Gas 2.

3 In a medium saucepan, heat the oil and garlic together for 1–2 minutes. Add the tomatoes and cook over a moderate to high heat until softened. Stir 175ml/6fl oz/¾ cup of the mussel cooking liquid into the saucepan.

4 Cook the pasta in plenty of boiling salted water until just *al dente*. Just before draining the pasta, add the prawns and parsley to the tomato sauce. Cook for 2 minutes. Taste for seasoning, adding salt and pepper if necessary. Remove from the heat.

5 Prepare four pieces of baking parchment paper or foil about 30 × 45cm/12 × 18in. Place each sheet in the centre of a shallow bowl. Turn the drained pasta into a mixing bowl. Add the tomato sauce and mix well. Stir in the mussels.

6 Divide the pasta and seafood among the four pieces of paper or foil, placing a mound in the centre of each, and twisting the ends together to make a closed packet. Arrange on a large baking sheet and place in the centre of the oven. Bake for 8–10 minutes. Place the unopened packets on individual serving plates.

Tagliatelle with Smoked Salmon

This is a pretty pasta dish with the light texture of the cucumber complementing the fish perfectly.

Serves 4

350g/12oz tagliatelle
½ cucumber
75g/3oz/6 tbsp butter
grated rind of 1 orange
30ml/2 tbsp chopped fresh dill
300ml/½ pint/1¼ cups single cream
15ml/1 tbsp orange juice
115g/4oz smoked salmon, skinned
salt and ground black pepper

1 Cook the pasta in plenty of boiling salted water according to the instructions on the packet.

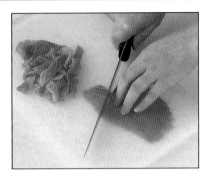

4 Melt the butter in a saucepan, add the orange rind and dill and stir well. Add the cucumber and cook gently for 2 minutes, stirring occasionally.

5 Add the cream and orange juice, and season to taste. Then simmer for 1 minute.

6 Meanwhile, cut the salmon into thin strips. Stir into the sauce and heat through.

7 Drain the pasta thoroughly and toss in the sauce until well coated. Serve immediately.

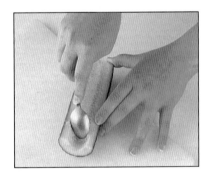

2 Using a sharp knife, cut the cucumber in half lengthways then, using a small spoon, scoop out the seeds and discard.

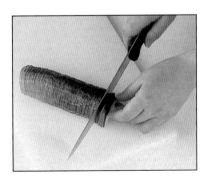

3 Turn the cucumber on the flat side and slice thinly.

Spaghetti with Clams

Try chopped fresh dill for a delicious alternative in this dish.

INGREDIENTS

Serves 4

24 live clams in the shell, scrubbed
250ml/8fl oz/1 cup water
120ml/4fl oz/½ cup dry white wine
450g/1lb spaghetti, preferably Italian
75ml/5 tbsp olive oil
2 garlic cloves, minced
45ml/3 tbsp chopped fresh parsley
salt and ground black pepper

1 Rinse the clams well in cold water and drain. Place in a large saucepan with the water and wine and bring to the boil. Cover and steam until the shells open, about 6–8 minutes.

2 Discard any clams that have not opened. Remove the clams from their shells. If large, chop them roughly.

3 Strain the cooking liquid through a strainer lined with muslin. Place in a small saucepan and boil rapidly until reduced by about half. Set aside.

4 Cook the spaghetti in plenty of boiling salted water according to the instructions on the packet until *al dente*.

5 Meanwhile, heat the olive oil in a large frying pan. Add the garlic and cook for 2–3 minutes, but do not let it brown. Add the reduced clam liquid and the parsley. Cook over a low heat until the spaghetti is ready.

6 Drain the spaghetti. Add to the frying pan, increase the heat to medium, and add the clams. Cook for 3–4 minutes, stirring, to coat the spaghetti with the sauce and to heat the clams.

7 Season with salt and pepper and serve at once.

Pasta with Prawns and Feta Cheese

This dish combines the richness of fresh prawns with the tartness of feta cheese. Goat's cheese could also be used, if preferred.

INGREDIENTS

Serves 4

450g/1lb raw prawns in the shell
6 spring onions
225g/8oz feta cheese
50g/2oz/4 tbsp butter
small bunch fresh chives
450g/1lb penne, garganelle or rigatoni
salt and ground black pepper

COOK'S TIP

If fresh prawns are not available, use well-thawed frozen, and add to the sauce at the last minute together with the spring onions.

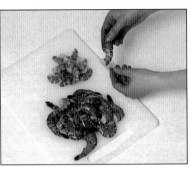

1 Remove the heads from the prawns by twisting and pulling off. Peel the prawns and discard the shells.

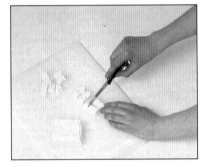

2 On a nylon chopping board, chop the spring onions and the feta cheese using a sharp knife.

3 Melt the butter in a frying pan and stir in the prawns. When they turn pink, add the spring onions and cook gently over a low heat for about 1 minute.

4 Stir the feta cheese into the prawn mixture and season with black pepper.

5 Snip the chives into 2.5cm/1in lengths and stir half into the prawn mixture.

6 Cook the pasta in plenty of boiling salted water according to the instructions on the packet. Drain well, pile into a warmed serving dish and top with the sauce. Scatter with the remaining chives and serve.

Fried Singapore Noodles

Thai fishcakes vary in their size and their spiciness. They are available from Oriental supermarkets.

INGREDIENTS

Serves 4

175g/6oz rice noodles

60ml/4 tbsp vegetable oil

2.5ml/½ tsp salt

75g/3oz/¾ cup cooked prawns

175g/6oz cooked pork, cut
   into matchsticks

1 green pepper, seeded and cut
   into matchsticks

2.5ml/½ tsp sugar

10ml/2 tsp curry powder

75g/3oz Thai fishcakes

10ml/2 tsp dark soy sauce

1 Soak the rice noodles in water for about 10 minutes, drain well through a colander, then pat dry with kitchen paper.

2 Heat a wok, then add half the oil. When the oil is hot, add the noodles and salt and stir-fry for 2 minutes. Transfer to a warmed serving dish and keep warm.

3 Heat the remaining oil and add the prawns, pork, pepper, sugar, curry powder and remaining salt. Stir-fry for 1 minute.

4 Return the noodles to the pan and stir-fry with the Thai fishcakes for 2 minutes. Stir in the soy sauce and serve immediately.

Prawns with Tagliatelle in Packets

A quick and impressive dish, easy to prepare in advance and cook at the last minute. When the paper packets are opened at the table, the filling smells wonderful.

INGREDIENTS

Serves 4

750g/1¾lb raw prawns in the shell

450g/1lb tagliatelle or similar pasta

150ml/¼ pint/⅔ cup fresh or ready-made
    pesto sauce

20ml/4 tsp olive oil

1 garlic clove, crushed

120ml/4fl oz/½ cup dry white wine

salt and ground black pepper

1 Preheat the oven to 200°C/ 400°F/Gas 6. Twist the heads off the prawns and discard.

2 Cook the tagliatelle in plenty of rapidly boiling salted water for 2 minutes only, then drain. Mix with half the pesto.

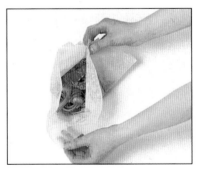

3 Cut four 30cm/12in squares of greaseproof paper and place 5ml/1 tsp olive oil in the centre of each. Pile equal amounts of pasta in the middle of each square.

4 Top with equal amounts of prawns and spoon over the remaining pesto mixed with the garlic. Season with pepper; sprinkle each with the wine.

5 Brush the edges of the paper lightly with water and bring them loosely up around the filling, twisting to enclose. (The parcels should look like money bags.)

6 Place the parcels on a baking sheet. Bake in the oven for 10–15 minutes. Serve at once, allowing the diners to open their own packets at the table.

Saffron Pappardelle

A wonderful dish with a delicious shellfish sauce.

Serves 4

large pinch saffron strands

4 sun-dried tomatoes, chopped

5ml/1 tsp fresh thyme

12 large prawns in their shells

225g/8oz baby squid

225g/8oz monkfish fillet

2–3 garlic cloves

2 small onions, quartered

1 small bulb fennel, trimmed and sliced

150ml/¼ pint/⅔ cup white wine

225g/8oz pappardelle

salt and ground black pepper

30ml/2 tbsp chopped fresh parsley,
   to garnish

1 Put the saffron, sun-dried tomatoes and thyme into a bowl with 60ml/4 tbsp hot water. Leave to soak for 30 minutes.

2 Wash the prawns and carefully remove the shells, leaving the heads and tails intact. Pull the body from the squid and remove the quill. Cut the tentacles from the head and rinse under cold water. Pull off the outer skin and cut into 5mm/¼in rings. Cut the monkfish into 2.5cm/1in cubes.

3 Put the garlic, onions and fennel into a pan with the wine. Cover and simmer for 5 minutes until tender.

4 Add the monkfish, saffron, tomatoes and thyme in their liquid. Cover and cook for 3 minutes. Then add the prawns and squid. Cover and cook gently for 1–2 minutes (do not overcook or the squid will become tough).

5 Meanwhile, cook the pasta in a large pan of boiling, salted water until *al dente*. Drain thoroughly.

6 Divide the pasta among four serving dishes and top with the fish and shellfish sauce. Sprinkle with parsley and serve at once.

Black Pasta with Scallops

A stunning pasta dish using black tagliatelle.

INGREDIENTS

Serves 4

120ml/4fl oz/½ cup low-fat crème fraîche

10ml/2 tsp wholegrain mustard

2 garlic cloves, crushed

30–45ml/2–3 tbsp fresh lime juice

60ml/4 tbsp chopped fresh parsley

30ml/2 tbsp snipped chives

350g/12oz black tagliatelle

12 large scallops

60ml/4 tbsp white wine

150ml/¼ pint/⅔ cup fish stock

salt and ground black pepper

lime wedges and parsley sprigs, to garnish

1 To make the tartare sauce, mix the crème fraîche, mustard, garlic, lime juice, herbs and seasoning together in a bowl.

2 Cook the pasta in a large pan of boiling, salted water until *al dente*. Drain thoroughly.

3 Slice the scallops in half horizontally. Keep any coral whole. Put the white wine and fish stock into a saucepan and heat to simmering point. Add the scallops and cook very gently for 3–4 minutes (no longer or they will become tough).

4 Remove the scallops. Boil the wine and stock to reduce by half and add the green sauce to the pan. Heat gently to warm, replace the scallops and cook gently for 1 minute. Spoon over the pasta and garnish with lime wedges and sprigs of parsley.

MEAT &
POULTRY
DISHES

~

Rotolo di Pasta

A giant Swiss roll of pasta with a spinach filling, which is poached, sliced and baked with béchamel or tomato sauce. Use fresh homemade pasta for this recipe, or ask your local Italian deli to make a large sheet of pasta for you!

INGREDIENTS

Serves 6

700g/1½lb frozen chopped
   spinach, thawed
50g/2oz/4 tbsp butter
1 onion, chopped
100g/4oz ham or bacon, diced
225g/8oz ricotta or curd cheese
1 egg
freshly grated nutmeg
fresh spinach pasta made with 2 eggs and
   200g/7oz/1¾ cups flour
1.2 litres/2 pints/5 cups béchamel
   sauce, warmed
50g/2oz/½ cup freshly grated
   Parmesan cheese
salt and ground black pepper

1 Squeeze the excess moisture from the spinach and set aside.

2 Melt the butter in a saucepan and fry the onion until golden. Add the ham and fry until beginning to brown. Take off the heat and stir in the spinach. Cool slightly, then beat in the ricotta or curd cheese and the egg. Season with salt, pepper and nutmeg.

3 Roll the pasta out to a rectangle about 30 × 40cm/12 × 16in. Spread the filling all over, leaving a 1cm/½in border all round the edge of the rectangle.

4 Roll up from the shorter end and wrap in muslin to form a "sausage", tying the ends securely with string. Poach in a very large pan (or fish kettle) of simmering water for 20 minutes or until firm. Carefully remove, drain and then unwrap. Leave to cool.

5 When you are ready to finish the dish, preheat the oven to 200°C/400°F/Gas 6. Cut the pasta roll into 2.5cm/1in slices. Spoon a little béchamel sauce over the base of a shallow baking dish and arrange the slices on top, slightly overlapping each other.

6 Spoon over the remaining sauce, sprinkle with the cheese and bake for 15–20 minutes or until browned and bubbling. Allow to stand for a few minutes before serving.

Macaroni with Ham and Tomato Sauce

This delicious dish can be cooked in moments and is absolutely perfect for entertaining unexpected guests.

INGREDIENTS

Serves 4

350g/12oz dried short-cut macaroni

45ml/3 tbsp olive oil

1 beefsteak tomato, chopped

1 clove garlic, chopped

175g/6oz cooked ham, cut into thick strips

175g/6oz goat's cheese, diced

3 tbsp fresh oregano leaves

salt and freshly ground black pepper

diced goat's cheese and oregano leaves, to garnish

1 Cook the pasta in a large pan of lightly salted, boiling water for 8–10 minutes, until tender but still firm to the bite.

2 Meanwhile, heat the oil in a large frying pan. Add the tomato, garlic and ham and sauté for 3 minutes.

COOK'S TIP

Goat's cheese is available in many forms, such as in herbed oil, coated with coarsely ground pepper and plain.

3 Lower the heat slightly, stir in the goat's cheese and oregano and simmer for a further 30 seconds. Season to taste with salt and pepper.

4 Drain the pasta thoroughly and toss with the sauce. Transfer to a warm serving dish and serve immediately, garnished with diced goat's cheese and oregano leaves.

Orechiette with Pork in Mustard Sauce

This country-style dish would taste even better made with wild mushrooms, such as ceps.

INGREDIENTS

Serves 4

350g/12 oz dried orechiette

60ml/4 tbsp olive oil

2 cloves garlic, chopped

350g/12oz pork fillet, thinly sliced

50g/2oz butter

175g/6oz open cap mushrooms, sliced

15ml/1 tbsp wholegrain mustard

45ml/3 tbsp snipped fresh chives

salt and freshly ground black pepper

snipped fresh chives, to garnish

1 Cook the pasta in a large saucepan of lightly salted, boiling water for approximately 8–10 minutes, until tender, but still firm to the bite.

2 Meanwhile, heat the oil in a large frying pan. Add the garlic and pork and fry, stirring occasionally, for 10 minutes, until the pork is browned and tender.

3 Add the butter, mushrooms and mustard and cook, stirring occasionally, for 2 minutes. Add the chives and season to taste with salt and pepper.

4 Meanwhile, drain the pasta thoroughly. Stir it into the pork mixture and cook for 1 minute, until heated through. Transfer to a warm serving dish, garnish with snipped fresh chives and serve immediately.

Tagliatelle with Prosciutto and Parmesan

This is a really simple dish, prepared in minutes from the best ingredients.

INGREDIENTS

Serves 4

115g/4oz prosciutto

450g/1lb tagliatelle

75g/3oz/6 tbsp butter

50g/2oz/½ cup freshly grated
   Parmesan cheese

salt and ground black pepper

a few fresh sage leaves, to garnish

1 Cut the prosciutto into strips the same width as the tagliatelle. Cook the pasta in plenty of boiling salted water according to the instructions on the packet.

2 Meanwhile, melt the butter gently in a saucepan, stir in the prosciutto strips and heat through over a very gentle heat, being careful not to fry.

3 Drain the tagliatelle through a colander and pile into a warmed serving dish.

4 Sprinkle over all the Parmesan cheese and pour over the buttery prosciutto. Season well with black pepper and garnish with the sage leaves.

Spaghetti with Meatballs

*No Italian menu would be complete
without meatballs. Serve these with
a light green salad if you like.*

INGREDIENTS

Serves 4

For the meatballs

1 onion, chopped

1 garlic clove, chopped

350g/12oz/3 cups minced lamb

1 egg yolk

15ml/1 tbsp dried mixed herbs

15ml/1 tbsp olive oil

salt and ground black pepper

For the sauce

300ml/½ pint/1¼ cups passata

30ml/2 tbsp chopped fresh basil

1 garlic clove, chopped

salt and ground black pepper

350g/12oz spaghetti

fresh rosemary sprigs, to garnish

freshly grated Parmesan cheese, to serve

1 To make the meatballs, mix
together the onion, garlic,
lamb, egg yolk, herbs and
seasoning until well blended.

2 Divide the mixture into about
20 pieces and mould into balls.
Place on a baking sheet, cover with
clear film and chill for at least
30 minutes.

3 Heat the oil in a large frying
pan and add the meatballs. Fry
for about 10 minutes, turning
occasionally, until browned.

4 Add the passata, basil, garlic
and seasoning to the pan and
bring to the boil. Cover and
simmer for 20 minutes, or until
the meatballs are tender.

5 Meanwhile, cook the pasta in
plenty of boiling salted water
according to the instructions on
the packet. Drain thoroughly and
divide among four serving plates.
Spoon over the meatballs and
some of the sauce. Garnish each
portion with a fresh rosemary
sprig and serve immediately with
plenty of freshly grated Parmesan
cheese handed separately.

Greek Pasta Bake

Another excellent main meal (called pastitsio in Greece), this recipe is both economical and filling.

INGREDIENTS

Serves 4

15ml/1 tbsp oil

450g/1lb/4 cups minced lamb

1 onion, chopped

2 garlic cloves, crushed

30ml/2 tbsp tomato purée

25g/1oz/2 tbsp plain flour

300ml/½ pint/1¼ cups lamb stock

2 large tomatoes

115g/4oz/1 cup pasta shapes

450g/1lb tub Greek yogurt

2 eggs

salt and ground black pepper

1 Preheat the oven to 190°C/ 375°F/Gas 5. Heat the oil in a large pan and fry the lamb for 5 minutes. Add the onion and garlic and continue to fry for a further 5 minutes.

2 Stir the tomato purée and flour into the pan. Cook for a further 1 minute.

3 Stir in the stock and season to taste. Bring to the boil and cook for 20 minutes.

4 Slice the tomatoes, place the meat in an ovenproof dish and arrange the tomatoes on top.

5 Cook the pasta shapes in boiling salted water for about 8–10 minutes or until *al dente*. Drain thoroughly.

6 Mix together the pasta, yogurt and eggs. Spoon on top of the tomatoes and then cook in the preheated oven for 1 hour. Serve with a crisp salad, if desired.

Bolognese Meat Sauce

This great meat sauce is a speciality of Bologna. It is delicious with tagliatelle or short pastas such as penne or conchiglie as well as spaghetti, and is indispensable in baked lasagne. It keeps well in the fridge for several days and can also be frozen for up to three months.

INGREDIENTS

Serves 6

25g/1oz/2 tbsp butter

60ml/4 tbsp olive oil

1 onion, finely chopped

25g/1oz/2 tbsp finely chopped pancetta or unsmoked bacon

1 carrot, finely sliced

1 celery stick, finely sliced

1 garlic clove, finely chopped

350g/12oz/3 cups lean minced beef

150ml/¼ pint/⅔ cup red wine

120ml/4fl oz/½ cup milk

400g/14oz can plum tomatoes, chopped, with their juice

1 bay leaf

1.5ml/¼ tsp fresh thyme leaves

salt and ground black pepper

cooked pasta, to serve

1 Heat the butter and oil in a heavy-based saucepan. Add the onion, and cook over a moderate heat for 3–4 minutes. Add the pancetta or bacon, and cook until the onion is translucent. Stir in the carrot, celery and garlic. Cook for a further 3–4 minutes.

2 Add the beef, and crumble it into the vegetables with a fork. Stir until the meat loses its red colour. Season to taste.

3 Pour in the wine, increase the heat slightly, and cook until the liquid evaporates, about 3–4 minutes. Add the milk and cook until it has evaporated.

4 Stir in the tomatoes with their juice, and the herbs. Bring the sauce to the boil. Reduce the heat to low and simmer, uncovered, for 1½–2 hours, stirring occasionally. Correct the seasoning before serving on a bed of pasta.

Baked Lasagne with Meat Sauce

This lasagne made from egg pasta with homemade meat and béchamel sauce is exquisite.

INGREDIENTS

Serves 8–10

2 quantities Bolognese Meat Sauce
egg pasta sheets made with 3 eggs or
    400g/14oz dried lasagne
115g/4oz/1 cup grated Parmesan cheese
40g/1½oz/3 tbsp butter

For the béchamel sauce

750ml/1¼ pints/3 cups milk
1 bay leaf
3 mace blades
115g/4oz/½ cup butter
75g/3oz/¾ cup plain flour
salt and ground black pepper

1 Prepare the meat sauce and set aside. Butter a large shallow baking dish, preferably rectangular or square.

COOK'S TIP

If you are using dried or bought pasta, follow step 4, but boil the lasagne in just two batches, and stop the cooking about 4 minutes before the recommended cooking time on the packet has elapsed. Rinse in cold water and lay the pasta out the same way as for the egg pasta.

2 Make the béchamel sauce by gently heating the milk with the bay leaf and mace in a small saucepan. Melt the butter in a medium heavy-based saucepan. Add the flour, and mix well with a wire whisk. Cook for 2–3 minutes. Strain the hot milk into the flour and butter, and mix smoothly with the whisk. Bring the sauce to the boil, stirring constantly, and cook for a further 4–5 minutes. Season with salt and pepper and set aside.

3 Make the pasta. Do not let it dry out before cutting it into rectangles measuring about 11cm/4½in wide and the same length as the baking dish (this will make it easier to assemble later). Preheat the oven to 200°C/400°F/Gas 6.

4 Bring a very large pan of water to the boil. Place a large bowl of cold water near the cooker. Cover a large work surface with a tablecloth. Add salt to the rapidly boiling water. Drop in 3 or 4 of the egg pasta rectangles. Cook very briefly, about 30 seconds. Remove from the pan, using a slotted spoon, and drop into the cold water for about 30 seconds. Pull them out of the water, shaking off the excess water. Lay them out flat without overlapping on the table-cloth. Continue with all the remaining pasta and trimmings.

5 To assemble the lasagne, spread one large spoonful of the meat sauce over the base of the dish. Arrange a layer of pasta in the dish, cutting it with a sharp knife so that it fits well.

6 Cover with a thin layer of meat sauce, then one of béchamel. Sprinkle with a little cheese. Repeat the layers in the same order, and ending with a layer of pasta coated with béchamel. Do not make more than about 6 layers of pasta. Use the pasta trimmings to patch any gaps in the pasta. Sprinkle the top with grated Parmesan cheese, and dot with butter.

7 Bake in the preheated oven for 20 minutes, or until brown on top. Remove from the oven and allow to stand for about 5 minutes before serving. Serve directly from the baking dish, cutting out rectangular or square sections for each helping.

Twin Cities Meatballs

Serve these meatballs without gravy as drinks party nibbles.

INGREDIENTS

Serves 6

30ml/2 tbsp butter or margarine

½ small onion, minced

350g/12oz/2¼ cups minced beef

115g/4oz/1 cup minced veal

225g/8oz/2 cups minced pork

1 egg

40g/1½oz/½ cup mashed potatoes

30ml/2 tbsp finely chopped fresh dill
   or parsley

1 garlic clove, crushed

5ml/1 tsp salt

2.5ml/½ tsp black pepper

2.5ml/½ tsp ground allspice

1.5ml/¼ tsp grated nutmeg

40g/1½oz/¾ cup fresh breadcrumbs

175ml/6fl oz/¾ cup milk

25g/1oz/¼ cup plain flour plus
   15ml/1 tbsp extra

30ml/2 tbsp olive oil

175ml/6fl oz/¾ cup evaporated milk

buttered noodles, to serve

1 Melt the butter or margarine in a large frying pan. Add the onion and cook over a low heat until softened, about 8–10 minutes. Remove from the heat. Using a slotted spoon, transfer the onion to a large mixing bowl.

2 Add the beef, veal and pork, the egg, mashed potatoes, dill or parsley, garlic, salt, pepper, allspice and nutmeg to the bowl.

3 Put the breadcrumbs in a small bowl and add the milk. Stir until well moistened, then add to the other ingredients. Mix well.

4 Shape the mixture into balls about 2.5cm/1in in diameter. Roll them in 25g/1oz/¼ cup of the flour to coat all over.

5 Add the olive oil to the frying pan and heat over a medium heat. Add the meatballs and brown on all sides for 8–10 minutes. Shake the pan occasionally to roll the balls so they colour evenly. With a slotted spoon, remove the meatballs to a serving dish. Cover with foil and keep warm.

6 Stir the 15ml/1 tbsp of flour into the fat in the frying pan. Add the evaporated milk and mix in with a small whisk. Simmer for 3–4 minutes. Check the seasoning, and adjust if necessary.

7 Pour the gravy over the meatballs. Serve hot with buttered noodles.

Pasta Timbales

An alternative way to serve pasta for a special occasion. Mixed with minced beef and tomato and baked in a lettuce parcel, it makes an impressive dish for a dinner party.

INGREDIENTS

Serves 4

8 cos lettuce leaves

For the filling
15ml/1 tbsp oil
175g/6oz/1½ cups minced beef
15ml/1 tbsp tomato purée
1 garlic clove, crushed
115g/4oz macaroni
salt and ground black pepper

For the sauce
25g/1oz/2 tbsp butter
25g/1oz/2 tbsp plain flour
250ml/8fl oz/1 cup double cream
30ml/2 tbsp chopped fresh basil

1 Preheat the oven to 180°C/350°F/Gas 4. For the filling, heat the oil in a large pan and fry the minced beef for 7 minutes. Add the tomato purée and garlic and cook for 5 minutes.

2 Cook the macaroni in boiling salted water for 8–10 minutes or until *al dente*. Drain.

3 Mix together the pasta and minced beef mixture.

4 Line four 150ml/¼ pint/⅔ cup ramekin dishes with the cos lettuce leaves. Season the mince and spoon into the lettuce-lined ramekins.

5 Fold the lettuce leaves over the filling and place in a roasting tin half-filled with boiling water. Cover and cook for 20 minutes.

6 For the sauce melt the butter in a pan. Add the flour and cook for 1 minute. Stir in the cream and fresh basil. Season and bring to the boil, stirring all the time. Turn out the timbales and serve with the creamy basil sauce, and a crisp green salad if liked.

Cannelloni Stuffed with Meat

Cannelloni are rectangles of home-made egg pasta which are spread with a filling, rolled up and baked in a sauce. In this recipe, they are baked in a béchamel sauce.

INGREDIENTS

Serves 6–8

30ml/2 tbsp olive oil

1 onion, very finely chopped

225g/8oz/1½ cups very lean minced beef

75g/3oz/½ cup finely chopped
   cooked ham

15ml/1 tbsp chopped fresh parsley

30ml/2 tbsp tomato purée, softened in
   15ml/1 tbsp warm water

1 egg

egg pasta sheets made with 2 eggs

750ml/1¼ pints/3 cups béchamel sauce

50g/2oz/½ cup freshly grated
   Parmesan cheese

40g/11/2oz/3 tbsp butter

salt and ground black pepper

1 Prepare the meat filling by heating the oil in a medium saucepan. Add the onion and sauté gently until translucent. Stir in the beef, crumbling it with a fork, and stirring constantly until it has lost its raw red colour. Cook for about 3–4 minutes.

2 Remove from the heat and turn the beef mixture into a bowl with the ham and parsley. Add the tomato purée mixture and the egg, and mix well. Season with salt and pepper. Set aside.

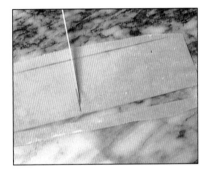

3 Make the egg pasta sheets. Do not let the pasta dry before cutting it into rectangles, about 13–15cm/5–6in long and as wide as they come from the machine (7.5cm/3in if you are not using a pasta machine).

4 Bring a very large pan of water to the boil. Place a large bowl of cold water near the cooker. Cover a large work surface with a tablecloth. Add salt to the rapidly boiling water. Drop in three or four of the egg pasta rectangles. Cook very briefly, for about 30 seconds. Plunge them into the cold water, shake off the excess and lay them out flat on the tablecloth. Continue until all the pasta has been cooked in this way.

5 Preheat the oven to 220°C/ 425°F/Gas 7. Select a shallow baking dish large enough to take all the cannelloni in one layer. Butter the dish and smear about 30–45ml/2–3 tbsp of béchamel sauce over the base.

6 Stir about one-third of the sauce into the meat filling. Spread a thin layer of filling on each pasta rectangle. Roll the rectangles up loosely starting from a long side, Swiss-roll style. Place the cannelloni in the baking dish with their open edges underneath.

7 Spoon the rest of the sauce over the cannelloni, pushing a little down between each pasta roll. Sprinkle the top with the grated Parmesan and dot with butter. Bake for about 20 minutes. Allow to rest for 5–8 minutes before serving on warmed plates.

Beef Strips with Orange and Ginger

Stir-frying is one of the quickest ways to cook, but you do need to choose tender meat.

INGREDIENTS

Serves 4

450g/1lb lean beef rump, fillet or sirloin, cut into thin strips

finely grated rind and juice of 1 orange

15ml/1 tbsp light soy sauce

5ml/1 tsp cornflour

2.5cm/1in piece fresh root ginger, finely chopped

10ml/2 tsp sesame oil

1 large carrot, cut into thin strips

2 spring onions, thinly sliced

rice noodles, to serve

1 Place the beef strips in a bowl and sprinkle over the orange rind and juice. Leave to marinate for at least 30 minutes.

2 Drain the liquid from the meat and reserve, then mix the meat with the soy sauce, cornflour and fresh root ginger.

3 Heat the oil in a wok or large frying pan and add the beef. Stir-fry for 1 minute until lightly coloured, then add the carrot and stir-fry for a further 2–3 minutes.

4 Stir in the spring onions and reserved liquid, then cook, stirring, until boiling and thickened. Serve the beef hot with rice noodles.

Piquant Chicken with Spaghetti

*The addition of cucumber and
tomatoes adds a deliciously fresh
flavour to this unusual dish.*

INGREDIENTS

Serves 4

1 onion, finely chopped

1 carrot, diced

1 garlic clove, crushed

300ml/½ pint/1¼ cups vegetable stock

4 chicken breasts, boned and skinned

1 bouquet garni

115g/4oz button mushrooms, thinly sliced

5ml/1 tsp wine vinegar or lemon juice

350g/12oz spaghetti

½ cucumber, peeled and cut into fingers

2 tomatoes, skinned, seeded and chopped

30ml/2 tbsp crème fraîche

15ml/1 tbsp chopped fresh parsley

15ml/1 tbsp snipped chives

salt and ground black pepper

1 Put the onion, carrot, garlic, stock, chicken and bouquet garni into a saucepan.

2 Bring to the boil, cover and simmer for 15–20 minutes or until the chicken is tender. Transfer the chicken to a plate and cover with foil.

3 Remove the chicken and strain the liquid. Discard the vegetables and return the liquid to the pan. Add the sliced mushrooms, wine vinegar or lemon juice and simmer for 2–3 minutes.

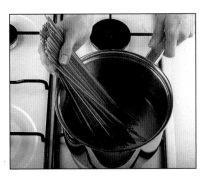

4 Cook the spaghetti in plenty of boiling salted water according to the instructions on the packet. Drain thoroughly.

5 Blanch the cucumber in boiling water for 10 seconds. Drain and rinse under cold water.

6 Cut the chicken breasts into bite-size pieces. Boil the stock to reduce by half, then add the chicken, tomatoes, crème fraîche, cucumber and herbs. Season with salt and pepper to taste.

7 Transfer the spaghetti to a warmed serving dish and spoon over the piquant chicken. Serve at once.

Chicken Cannelloni al Forno

A lighter alternative to the usual beef-filled, béchamel-coated version. Fill with ricotta cheese, onion and mushroom for a vegetarian version.

INGREDIENTS

Serves 4–6

450g/1lb skinless, boneless chicken
   breast, cooked
225g/8oz mushrooms
2 garlic cloves, crushed
30ml/2 tbsp chopped fresh parsley
15ml/1 tbsp chopped fresh tarragon
1 egg, beaten
freshly squeezed lemon juice
12–18 cannelloni tubes
400g/14oz jar tomato pasta sauce
50g/2oz/½ cup freshly grated
   Parmesan cheese
salt and ground black pepper
fresh parsley sprig, to garnish

1 Preheat the oven to 200°C/ 400°F/Gas 6. Place the chicken in a blender or food processor and process until finely minced. Transfer to a bowl.

2 Place the mushrooms, garlic, parsley and tarragon in the blender or food processor and process until finely minced.

3 Beat the mushroom mixture into the chicken with the egg, salt and ground black pepper and lemon juice to taste.

4 If necessary, cook the cannelloni in plenty of salted boiling water according to the instructions on the packet. Drain well and pat dry on a clean dish towel.

5 Place the filling in a piping bag fitted with a large plain nozzle. Use to fill each tube of cannelloni.

6 Lay the filled cannelloni tightly together in a single layer in a buttered shallow ovenproof dish. Spoon over the tomato sauce and sprinkle with Parmesan cheese. Bake in the oven for 30 minutes or until brown and bubbling. Serve the cannelloni garnished with a sprig of parsley.

Chicken Lasagne

Based on the Italian beef lasagne, this is an excellent dish for entertaining guests of all ages. Serve simply with a green salad.

INGREDIENTS

INGREDIENTS

Serves 8

30ml/2 tbsp olive oil

900g/2lb/8 cups minced raw chicken

225g/8oz rindless streaky bacon
    rashers, chopped

2 garlic cloves, crushed

450g/1lb leeks, sliced

225g/8oz carrots, diced

30ml/2 tbsp tomato purée

450ml/¾ pint/1¾ cups chicken stock

12 sheets (no-precook) green lasagne

For the cheese sauce

50g/2oz/4 tbsp butter

50g/2oz/4 tbsp plain flour

600ml/1 pint/2½ cups milk

115g/4oz/1 cup grated mature
    Cheddar cheese

1.5ml/¼ tsp English mustard powder

salt and ground black pepper

1 Heat the oil in a large flame-proof casserole and brown the minced chicken and bacon briskly, separating the pieces with a wooden spoon. Add the crushed garlic cloves, chopped leeks and diced carrots and cook for about 5 minutes until softened. Add the tomato purée, stock and seasoning. Bring to the boil, cover and simmer for 30 minutes.

2 For the sauce, melt the butter in a saucepan, add the flour and gradually blend in the milk, stirring until smooth. Bring to the boil, stirring all the time until thickened, and simmer for several minutes. Add half the grated Cheddar cheese and the mustard and season to taste.

3 Preheat the oven to 190°C/ 375°F/Gas 5. Layer the chicken mixture, lasagne and half the cheese sauce in a 2.5 litre/5 pint/12 cup ovenproof dish, starting and finishing with the chicken mixture.

4 Pour over the remaining cheese sauce, sprinkle over the remaining cheese and bake in the preheated oven for 1 hour, or until lightly browned.

Noodles with Chicken, Prawns and Ham

Unlike most other kinds of noodles, egg noodles can be cooked up to 24 hours in advance and kept in a bowl of cold water in the refrigerator until required.

INGREDIENTS

Serves 4–6

275g/10oz dried egg noodles

15ml/1 tbsp vegetable oil

1 medium onion, chopped

1 clove garlic, crushed

2.5cm/1in piece fresh root
    ginger, chopped

50g/2oz canned water chestnuts, drained,
    rinsed and sliced

15ml/1 tbsp light soy sauce

30ml/2 tbsp fish sauce or strong
    chicken stock

175g/6oz cooked boneless chicken breast,
    thinly sliced

150g/5oz cooked ham, thickly sliced and
    cut into short fingers

225g/8oz cooked prawns, peeled

175g/6oz beansprouts

200g/7oz can baby corn cobs,
    drained

2 limes, cut into wedges, and 1 small
    bunch coriander, shredded,
    to garnish

1 Cook the noodles according to the packet instructions. Drain well and set aside.

2 Heat the oil in a preheated wok or heavy-based frying pan. Add the onion, garlic and ginger and stir-fry for 3 minutes, until the onion is soft but not coloured. Add the chestnuts, soy sauce, fish sauce or chicken stock, chicken breast, ham and prawns.

3 Add the drained egg noodles, beansprouts and baby corn cobs and stir-fry for about 6–8 minutes, until thoroughly heated through. Transfer to a warm serving dish, garnish with the lime wedges and shredded coriander and serve immediately.

Stir-fried Sweet and Sour Chicken

There are few cookery concepts that are better suited to today's busy lifestyle than the all-in-one stir-fry. This one has a wonderful South-east Asian influence.

INGREDIENTS

Serves 4

275g/10oz Chinese egg noodles
30ml/2 tbsp vegetable oil
3 spring onions, chopped
1 garlic clove, crushed
2.5cm/1in piece fresh root ginger, peeled
    and grated
5ml/1 tsp hot paprika
5ml/1 tsp ground coriander
3 boneless chicken breasts, sliced
115g/4oz/1 cup sugar-snap peas, topped
    and tailed
115g/4oz baby sweetcorn, halved
225g/8oz fresh beansprouts
15ml/1 tbsp cornflour
45ml/3 tbsp soy sauce
45ml/3 tbsp lemon juice
15ml/1 tbsp sugar
45ml/3 tbsp chopped fresh coriander or
    spring onion tops, to garnish

1 Bring a large saucepan of salted water to the boil. Add the noodles and cook according to the instructions on the packet. Drain, cover and keep warm.

2 Heat the oil in a wok. Add the spring onions and cook over a gentle heat. Mix in the next five ingredients, then stir-fry for about 3–4 minutes. Add the next three ingredients and steam briefly. Add the noodles.

3 Combine the cornflour, soy sauce, lemon juice and sugar in a small bowl. Add to the wok and simmer briefly to thicken. Serve garnished with chopped coriander or spring onion tops.

VEGETARIAN
DISHES

~

Pasta with Caponata

*The Sicilians have an excellent
sweet-and-sour vegetable dish,
called* caponata, *which goes
wonderfully well with pasta.*

INGREDIENTS

Serves 4

1 aubergine, cut into sticks

2 courgettes, cut into sticks

8 baby onions, peeled or 1 large
    onion, sliced

2 garlic cloves, crushed

1 large red pepper, sliced

60ml/4 tbsp olive oil, preferably
    extra virgin

450ml/¾ pint/1¾ cups tomato juice

150ml/¼ pint/⅔ cup water

30ml/2 tbsp balsamic vinegar

juice of 1 lemon

15ml/1 tbsp sugar

30ml/2 tbsp sliced black olives

30ml/2 tbsp capers

400g/14oz tagliatelle or other
    ribbon pasta

salt and ground black pepper

1 Lightly salt the aubergine and
courgettes and leave them to
drain in a colander for 30 minutes.
Rinse and pat dry thoroughly with
kitchen paper.

2 In a large saucepan, lightly fry
the onions, garlic and pepper
in the oil for 5 minutes, then stir in
the aubergine and courgettes and
fry for a further 5 minutes.

3 Stir in the tomato juice and the
water. Stir well, bring the
mixture to the boil, then add all
the rest of the ingredients except
the pasta. Season to taste and
simmer for 10 minutes.

4 Meanwhile, cook the pasta
according to the instructions
on the packet, then drain. Serve
the *caponata* with the pasta.

Aubergine Lasagne

This delicious lasagne is also suitable for home freezing.

INGREDIENTS

Serves 4

3 aubergines, sliced

75ml/5 tbsp olive oil

2 large onions, finely chopped

2 × 400g/14oz cans chopped tomatoes

5ml/1 tsp dried mixed herbs

2–3 garlic cloves, crushed

6 sheets no-precook lasagne

salt and ground black pepper

For the cheese sauce

25g/1oz/2 tbsp butter

25g/1oz/2 tbsp plain flour

300ml/½ pint/1¼ cups milk

2.5ml/½ tsp English mustard

115g/4oz/8 tbsp grated mature Cheddar

15g/½oz/1 tbsp grated Parmesan cheese

1 Layer the sliced aubergine in a colander, sprinkling lightly with salt between each layer. Leave to stand for 1 hour, then rinse and pat dry with kitchen paper.

2 Heat 60ml/4 tbsp of the oil in a large pan, fry the aubergine and drain on kitchen paper. Add the remaining oil to the pan, cook the onions for 5 minutes, then stir in the tomatoes, herbs, garlic and seasoning. Bring to the boil and simmer, covered, for 30 minutes.

3 Melt the butter in a pan, stir in the flour and cook gently for 1 minute, stirring. Gradually stir in the milk. Bring to the boil, stirring, and cook for 2 minutes. Remove from the heat and stir in the mustard, cheeses and seasoning.

4 Preheat the oven to 200°C/ 400°F/Gas 6. Arrange half the aubergines in the base of an ovenproof dish, spoon over half the tomato sauce. Arrange three sheets of lasagne on top. Repeat.

5 Spoon over the cheese sauce, cover and bake for 30 minutes until lightly browned.

Spaghetti with Mixed Mushrooms

This combination of mixed mushrooms and freshly chopped sweet basil tossed with spaghetti would be well complemented by a simple tomato salad.

INGREDIENTS

Serves 4

50g/2oz/¼ cup butter

1 onion, chopped

350g/12oz spaghetti

350g/12oz mixed mushrooms, such as
    brown, flat and button, sliced

1 garlic clove, chopped

300ml/½ pint/1¼ cups soured cream

30ml/2 tbsp chopped fresh basil

50g/2oz/½ cup freshly grated
    Parmesan cheese

salt and ground black pepper

torn flat leaf parsley, to garnish

freshly grated Parmesan cheese, to serve

1 Melt the butter in a large frying pan and fry the chopped onion for 10 minutes until softened.

2 Cook the pasta in plenty of boiling salted water according to the instructions on the packet.

3 Stir the mushrooms and garlic into the onion mixture and fry for 10 minutes until softened.

4 Add the soured cream, basil, grated Parmesan cheese and salt and pepper to taste. Cover and heat through.

5 Drain the pasta thoroughly and toss with the sauce. Serve immediately, garnished with torn flat leaf parsley, with plenty of grated Parmesan cheese.

Tortelli with Pumpkin Stuffing

During autumn and winter the northern Italian markets are full of bright orange pumpkins which are used to make soups and pasta dishes. This flavoursome dish is a speciality of Mantua.

INGREDIENTS

Serves 6-8

1kg/2¼lb pumpkin (weight with shell)

75g/3oz/1½ cups amaretti
  biscuits, crushed

2 eggs

75g/3oz/¾ cup freshly grated
  Parmesan cheese

pinch of grated nutmeg

plain breadcrumbs, as required

egg pasta sheets made with 3 eggs

salt and ground black pepper

To serve

115g/4oz/½ cup butter

75g/3oz/¾ cup freshly grated
  Parmesan cheese

1 Preheat the oven to 190°C/
375°F/Gas 5. Then cut the pumpkin into 10cm/4in pieces, leaving the skin on. Place the pumpkin pieces in a covered casserole and bake for about 45–50 minutes. When cool, cut off the skins. Purée the flesh in a food mill, blender or food processor or press through a sieve with a wooden spoon.

2 Combine the pumpkin purée with the biscuit crumbs, eggs, Parmesan and nutmeg. Season with salt and pepper. If the mixture is too wet, add about 15–30ml/1–2 tbsp breadcrumbs. Set aside until required.

3 Prepare the sheets of egg pasta. Roll out very thinly by hand or machine. Do not let the pasta dry out before filling.

4 Place tablespoonfuls of filling every 6cm/2½in along the pasta in rows 5cm/2in apart. Cover with another sheet of pasta, and press down gently. Use a fluted pastry or pasta wheel to cut between the rows to form rectangles with filling in the centre of each. Place the tortelli on a lightly floured surface, and allow to dry for at least 30 minutes, turning occasionally to dry both sides.

5 Bring a large pan of salted water to the boil. Gently heat the butter over a very low heat, taking care that it does not darken.

6 Drop the tortelli into the boiling water. Stir to prevent them from sticking. They will be cooked in 4–5 minutes. Drain and arrange in individual dishes. Spoon over the melted butter, sprinkle with grated Parmesan cheese and serve at once.

Magnificent Marrow

At autumn time, marrows – with their wonderful green and cream stripes – look so attractive and tempting. They make delicious, inexpensive main courses, just right for a satisfying family meal.

INGREDIENTS

Serves 4–6

250g/9oz pasta shells

1.5–1.75kg/3–4½lb marrow

1 onion, chopped

1 pepper, seeded and chopped

15ml/1 tbsp fresh root ginger, grated

2 garlic cloves, crushed

45ml/3 tbsp sunflower oil

4 large tomatoes, skinned and chopped

50g/2oz/½ cup pine nuts

15ml/1 tbsp chopped fresh basil

salt and ground black pepper

grated cheese, to serve (optional)

1 Preheat the oven to 190°C/375°F/Gas 5. Cook the pasta in plenty of boiling salted water according to the instructions on the packet, slightly overcooking it so it is just a little soft. Drain well and reserve.

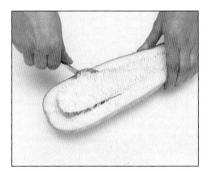

2 Cut the marrow in half lengthways and scoop out and discard the seeds. Use a small sharp knife and tablespoon to scoop out the marrow flesh. Chop the flesh roughly.

3 Gently fry the onion, pepper, ginger and garlic in the oil for 5 minutes then add the marrow flesh, tomatoes and seasoning. Cover and cook for 10–12 minutes until the vegetables are soft.

4 Add the pasta, pine nuts and basil to the pan, stir well and set aside until required.

5 Meanwhile, place the marrow halves in a roasting tin, season lightly and pour a little water around the marrow, taking care it does not spill inside. Cover with foil and bake for 15 minutes.

6 Remove the foil, discard the water and fill the shells with the vegetable mixture. Cover with foil and return to the oven for a further 20–25 minutes.

7 Top with cheese, if using. To serve, scoop out of the "shell" or cut into sections.

Coriander Ravioli with Pumpkin Filling

This stunning herb pasta is served with a superb creamy pumpkin and roast garlic filling.

INGREDIENTS

Serves 4–6

200g/7oz/scant 1 cup strong white flour

2 eggs

pinch of salt

45ml/3 tbsp chopped fresh coriander

coriander sprigs, to garnish

For the filling

4 garlic cloves, unpeeled

450g/1lb pumpkin, peeled and seeded

115g/4oz/½ cup ricotta cheese

4 sun-dried tomatoes in olive oil, drained
    and finely chopped, and
    30ml/2 tbsp of the oil

ground black pepper

1 Place the flour, eggs, salt and chopped fresh coriander into a blender or food processor and pulse until combined.

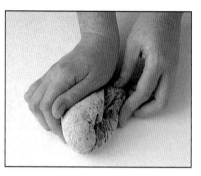

2 Place the dough on a lightly floured board and knead well for 5 minutes, until smooth. Wrap in clear film and leave to rest in the fridge for 20 minutes.

3 Preheat the oven to 200°C/ 400°F/Gas 6. Place the garlic cloves on a baking sheet and bake for 10 minutes until soft. Steam the pumpkin for 5–8 minutes until tender and drain well. Peel the garlic cloves and mash into the pumpkin together with the ricotta cheese and drained sun-dried tomatoes. Season with lots of ground black pepper.

4 Divide the pasta into four pieces and flatten slightly. Using a pasta machine, on its thinnest setting, roll out each piece. Leave the sheets of pasta on a clean dish towel until they are slightly dried.

5 Using a 7.5cm/3in crinkle-edged round cutter, stamp out 36 rounds of pasta.

6 Top 18 of the rounds with a teaspoonful of filling, brush the edges with water and place another round of pasta on top. Press firmly around the edges to seal. Bring a large pan of water to the boil, add the ravioli and cook for 3–4 minutes. Drain well and toss into the reserved tomato oil. Serve at once garnished with fresh coriander sprigs.

Autumn Glory

Glorious pumpkin shells summon up the delights of autumn and seem too good simply to throw away. Use one instead as a serving dish. Pumpkin and pasta make marvellous partners, especially as a main course served from the baked shell.

INGREDIENTS

Serves 4

1.75kg/4–4½lb pumpkin
1 onion, sliced
2.5cm/1in piece fresh root ginger
45ml/3 tbsp extra virgin olive oil
1 courgette, sliced
115g/4oz sliced mushrooms
400g/14oz can chopped tomatoes
75g/3oz pasta shells
450ml/¾ pint/1¾ cups stock
60ml/4 tbsp fromage frais
30ml/2 tbsp chopped fresh basil
salt and ground black pepper

1 Preheat the oven to 180°C/ 350°F/Gas 4. Cut the top off the pumpkin with a large, sharp knife and scoop out and discard the pumpkin seeds.

2 Using a small sharp knife and a sturdy tablespoon, cut and scrape out as much flesh from the pumpkin shell as possible, then chop the flesh into rough chunks.

3 Bake the pumpkin with its lid on for 45 minutes–1 hour until the inside begins to soften.

4 Meanwhile, make the filling. Gently fry the onion, ginger and pumpkin flesh in the olive oil for about 10 minutes, stirring the mixture occasionally.

5 Add the sliced courgette and mushrooms and cook for a further 3 minutes, then stir in the tomatoes, pasta shells and stock. Season well, bring to the boil, then cover the pan and simmer gently for about 10 minutes.

6 Stir the fromage frais and basil into the pasta and spoon the mixture into the pumpkin. It may not be possible to fit all the filling into the pumpkin shell, so serve the rest separately if necessary.

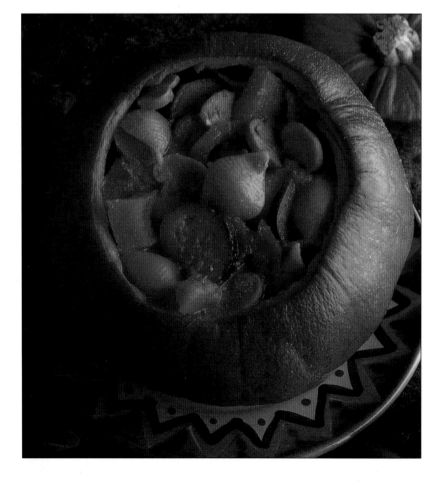

Stuffed Pasta Half-moons

These stuffed egg pasta half-moons are filled with a delicate mixture of cheeses. They make an elegant first course as well as a good supper.

INGREDIENTS

Serves 6–8

225g/8oz/1¼ cups fresh ricotta or
    curd cheese
225g/8oz/1¼ cups mozzarella cheese
115g/4oz/1 cup freshly grated
    Parmesan cheese
2 eggs
45ml/3 tbsp finely chopped fresh basil
salt and ground black pepper
egg pasta sheets made with 3 eggs

For the sauce
450g/1lb fresh tomatoes
30ml/2 tbsp olive oil
1 small onion, very finely chopped
90ml/6 tbsp cream

1 Press the ricotta or curd cheese through a sieve or strainer. Chop the mozzarella into very small cubes. Combine all three cheeses in a bowl. Beat in the eggs and basil, season and set aside.

2 Make the sauce by dropping the tomatoes into a small pan of boiling water for 1 minute. Remove, and peel using a small sharp knife to pull off the skins. Chop the tomatoes finely. Heat the oil in a medium saucepan. Add the onion and cook over a moderate heat until soft and translucent. Add the tomatoes and cook until soft, about 15 minutes. Season with salt and pepper. (The sauce may be pressed through a sieve to make it smooth.) Set aside.

3 Prepare the sheets of egg pasta. Roll out very thinly by hand or machine. Do not let the pasta dry out before filling.

4 Using a glass or pastry cutter, cut out rounds approximately 10cm/4in in diameter. Spoon one large tablespoon of the cheese filling on to one half of each pasta round and fold over.

5 Press the edges closed with a fork. Re-roll any trimmings and use to make more rounds. Allow the half-moons to dry for at least 10–15 minutes. Turn them over so they dry evenly.

6 Bring a large pan of salted water to the boil. Meanwhile, place the tomato sauce in a small saucepan and heat gently. Stir in the cream. Do not allow to boil.

7 Gently drop in the stuffed pasta, and stir carefully to prevent them from sticking. Cook for 5–7 minutes. Scoop them out of the water, drain carefully, and arrange in individual dishes. Spoon on some sauce to serve.

Baked Vegetable Lasagne

Following the principles of the classic meat sauce lasagne, other combinations of ingredients can be used most effectively. This vegetarian lasagne uses tomatoes and wild and cultivated mushrooms.

INGREDIENTS

Serves 8

egg pasta sheets made with 3 eggs

30ml/2 tbsp olive oil

1 onion, very finely chopped

500g/1¼lb tomatoes, fresh or
    canned, chopped

salt and ground black pepper

675g/1½lb cultivated or wild mushrooms,
    or a combination of both

75g/3oz/⅓ cup butter

2 garlic cloves, finely chopped

juice of ½ lemon

1 litre/1¾ pints/4 cups béchamel sauce

175g/6oz/1½ cups freshly grated
    Parmesan or Cheddar cheese, or a
    combination of both

1 Butter a large shallow baking
dish, preferably rectangular or
square in shape.

2 Make the egg pasta. Do not let
it dry out before cutting into
rectangles measuring about
11cm/4½in wide and the same
length as the baking dish (this will
make it easier to assemble).

3 In a small frying pan heat the
oil and sauté the onion until
translucent. Add the chopped
tomatoes and cook for about
6–8 minutes, stirring often. Season
with salt and pepper and set aside
until required.

4 Wipe the mushrooms carefully
with a damp cloth. Slice finely.
Heat 40g/1½oz/3 tbsp of the butter
in a frying pan and, when it is
bubbling, add the mushrooms.
Cook until the mushrooms start to
exude their juices. Add the garlic
and lemon juice, and season with
salt and pepper. Cook until the
liquids have almost all evaporated
and the mushrooms are starting to
brown. Set aside.

5 Preheat the oven to 200°C/
400°F/Gas 6. Bring a very large
pan of water to the boil. Place a
large bowl of cold water near the
cooker. Cover a large work surface
with a tablecloth. Add salt to the
rapidly boiling water. Drop in
three or four of the egg pasta
rectangles. Cook very briefly, about
30 seconds. Remove from the pan
using a slotted spoon and then
drop into the cold water for
about 30 seconds. Remove and
lay out to dry. Continue with the
remaining pasta.

6 To assemble the lasagne,
spread one large spoonful of
the béchamel sauce over the base
of the dish. Arrange a layer of pasta
in the dish, cutting it with a sharp
knife to fit. Cover with a thin layer
of mushrooms, then one of
béchamel sauce. Sprinkle with a
little cheese.

7 Make another layer of pasta,
spread with a thin layer of
tomatoes, and then one of
béchamel. Sprinkle with cheese.
Repeat the layers in the same
order, ending with a layer of pasta
coated with béchamel. Do not
make more than about six layers of
pasta. Use the pasta trimmings to
patch any gaps in the pasta.
Sprinkle with more cheese and dot
with butter.

8 Bake for 20 minutes. Remove
from the oven and allow to
stand for 5 minutes before serving.

Leek and Chèvre Lasagne

An unusual and lighter than average lasagne using a soft French goat's cheese. The pasta sheets are not so chewy if boiled briefly first, or you could use no-precook lasagne instead if you prefer.

<hr>

INGREDIENTS

Serves 6

6–8 lasagne sheets

1 large aubergine, sliced

3 leeks, thinly sliced

30ml/2 tbsp olive oil

2 red peppers, roasted

200g/7oz chèvre, broken into pieces

50g/2oz/½ cup freshly grated pecorino or Parmesan cheese

For the sauce

65g/2½oz/9 tbsp plain flour

65g/2½oz/5 tbsp butter

900ml/1½ pints/3¾ cups milk

2.5ml/½ tsp ground bay leaves

freshly grated nutmeg

salt and ground black pepper

1 Blanch the pasta sheets in plenty of boiling water for just 2 minutes. Drain and place on a clean dish towel.

2 Lightly salt the aubergine slices and place in a colander to drain for 30 minutes, then rinse and pat dry with kitchen paper.

3 Preheat the oven to 190°C/ 375°F/Gas 5. Lightly fry the leeks in the oil for 5 minutes, until softened. Peel the roasted peppers and cut into strips.

4 To make the sauce, put the flour, butter and milk into a saucepan and bring to the boil, stirring constantly until thickened. Add the ground bay leaves, nutmeg and seasoning. Simmer the sauce for a further 2 minutes.

5 In a greased shallow casserole, layer the leeks, lasagne sheets, aubergine, chèvre and pecorino or Parmesan. Trickle the sauce over the layers, ensuring that plenty goes in-between.

6 Finish with a layer of sauce and grated cheese. Bake in the oven for 30 minutes, or until bubbling and browned on top. Serve immediately.

Pasta with Roasted Vegetables

Sweet roasted vegetables form the basis of a rich sauce.

INGREDIENTS

Serves 4

1 large onion

1 aubergine

2 courgettes

2 peppers, preferably red or yellow, seeded

450g/1lb tomatoes, preferably plum

2–3 garlic cloves, coarsely chopped

60ml/4 tbsp olive oil

300ml/½ pint/1¼ cups smooth
 tomato sauce

50g/2oz black olives, stoned and halved

375–450g/12oz–1lb dried penne

salt and ground black pepper

15g/½oz fresh basil, shredded, to garnish

freshly grated Parmesan or pecorino
 cheese, to serve

1 Preheat the oven to 240°C/ 475°F/Gas 9. Cut the onion, aubergine, courgettes, peppers and tomatoes into 2.5–4cm/1–1½in chunks. Scoop out and discard the tomato seeds.

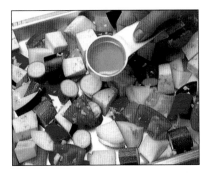

2 Spread out the vegetables in a large roasting tin. Sprinkle the garlic and oil over the vegetables and stir and turn to mix evenly. Season with salt and pepper.

3 Roast the vegetables for about 30 minutes or until they are soft and browned (don't worry if the edges are charred black). Stir after 15 minutes.

4 Scrape the vegetable mixture into a saucepan. Add the tomato sauce and olives.

5 Cook the pasta in plenty of boiling salted water, according to the instructions on the packet, until *al dente*.

6 Meanwhile, heat the tomato and roasted vegetable sauce. Taste and adjust the seasoning if necessary.

7 Drain the pasta and return to the pan. Add the tomato and roasted vegetable sauce and stir to mix well. Serve hot, sprinkled with the basil. If you like, serve with freshly grated Parmesan or pecorino cheese handed separately.

Penne with Aubergine and Mint Pesto

This splendid variation on the classic Italian pesto uses fresh mint rather than basil for a deliciously different flavour.

INGREDIENTS

Serves 4

2 large aubergines

450g/1lb penne

50g/2oz/½ cup walnut halves

salt and ground black pepper

For the pesto

25g/1oz fresh mint

15g/½oz flat leaf parsley

40g/1½oz/scant ½ cup walnuts

40g/1½oz finely grated Parmesan cheese

2 garlic cloves

90ml/6 tbsp olive oil

1 Cut the aubergines lengthways into 1cm/½in slices.

2 Cut the slices again crossways to give short strips.

3 Layer the strips in a colander with salt and leave to stand for 30 minutes over a plate to catch any juices. Rinse well in cool water and then drain thoroughly.

4 Place all the pesto ingredients, except the oil, in a blender or food processor. Blend until very smooth, then gradually add the oil in a thin stream until the mixture amalgamates. Season to taste.

5 Cook the penne in plenty of boiling salted water according to the instructions on the packet for about 8 minutes or until *al dente*. Add the aubergine and cook for a further 3 minutes.

6 Drain the pasta well and mix in the mint pesto and walnut halves. Serve immediately.

Macaroni Soufflé

This is generally a great favourite with children, and is rather like a light and fluffy macaroni cheese. Make sure you serve the soufflé immediately after it is cooked or it will sink dramatically.

INGREDIENTS

Serves 3–4

75g/3oz short cut macaroni
melted butter, to coat
25g/1oz/3 tbsp dried breadcrumbs
50g/2oz/4 tbsp butter
5ml/1 tsp ground paprika
40g/1½oz/⅓ cup plain flour
300ml/½ pint/1¼ cups milk
75g/3oz Cheddar or Gruyère
    cheese, grated
50g/2oz Parmesan cheese, grated
3 eggs, separated
salt and ground black pepper

1 Cook the macaroni in plenty of boiling salted water according to the instructions on the packet. Drain well and set aside. Preheat the oven to 150°C/300°F/Gas 2.

2 Brush a 1.2 litre/2 pint/5 cup soufflé dish with melted butter, then coat evenly with the bread-crumbs, shaking out any excess from the pan.

3 Put the butter, paprika, flour and milk into a saucepan and slowly bring to the boil, whisking constantly until the mixture is smooth and thick.

4 Simmer the sauce for 1 minute, then remove from the heat and stir in the cheeses until melted. Season well and mix with the cooked macaroni.

5 Beat in the egg yolks. Whisk the egg whites until they form soft peaks and spoon a quarter into the sauce mixture to lighten it slightly.

6 Using a large metal spoon, carefully fold in the rest of the egg whites and transfer to the prepared soufflé dish.

7 Bake in the centre of the oven for about 40–45 minutes until the soufflé is risen and golden brown. The middle should wobble very slightly and the soufflé should be lightly creamy inside.

Ravioli with Cheese and Herbs

Vary the herbs according to what you have to hand.

Serves 4–6

225g/8oz/1 cup full-fat soft
   cheese, softened
1 garlic clove, finely chopped
25g/1oz mixed herbs, such as thyme, basil,
   chives and parsley, finely chopped
1 quantity fresh pasta dough, rolled by
   machine into 2 x 30cm/12in strips, or
   divided into 4 and rolled by hand as
   thinly as possible
semolina, to coat
115g/4oz/½ cup butter
salt and ground black pepper

1 Mix together the soft cheese, garlic and most of the herbs. Season with salt and pepper.

2 Make the ravioli, filling them with the cheese and herb mixture. Toss the ravioli in a little semolina to coat lightly and leave to rest at room temperature for about 15 minutes.

3 Bring a large pan of salted water to the boil. Drop in the ravioli and cook for 7–9 minutes or until they are just tender to the bite. Drain well.

4 Melt the butter. Toss the ravioli in the melted butter. Sprinkle with the remaining herbs and serve immediately.

VARIATION

For Ravioli with Gorgonzola and Pine Nuts, fill the ravioli with a mixture of 115g/4oz/½ cup each full-fat soft cheese and crumbled Gorgonzola cheese; omit the garlic and herbs. Sprinkle the cooked ravioli with 25g/1oz/¼ cup toasted pine nuts instead of herbs.

Baked Tortellini with Three Cheeses

Serve this straight out of the oven while the cheese is still runny. If smoked mozzarella cheese is not available, try using a smoked German cheese or even grated smoked Cheddar.

INGREDIENTS

Serves 4–6

450g/1lb fresh tortellini

2 eggs

350g/12oz/1½ cups ricotta or curd cheese

25g/1oz/2 tbsp butter

25g/1oz fresh basil leaves

115g/4oz smoked mozzarella cheese

60ml/4 tbsp freshly grated
   Parmesan cheese

salt and ground black pepper

1 Preheat the oven to 190°C/ 375°F/Gas 5. Cook the fresh tortellini in plenty of boiling salted water according to the instructions on the packet. Drain well.

2 Beat the eggs with the ricotta or curd cheese and season well with salt and pepper. Use the butter to grease an ovenproof dish. Spoon in half the tortellini, pour over half the cheese mixture and cover with half the basil leaves.

3 Cover with the mozzarella and remaining basil. Top with the rest of the tortellini and spread over the remaining ricotta or curd cheese mixture.

4 Sprinkle evenly with the Parmesan cheese. Bake in the oven for 35–45 minutes or until golden brown and bubbling.

SALADS

~

Pasta Salad with Olives

This delicious salad combines all the flavours of the Mediterranean. It is an excellent way of serving pasta and is particularly suitable for a hot summer's day.

INGREDIENTS

Serves 6

450g/1lb short pasta, such as medium
   shells, farfalle or penne
60ml/4 tbsp extra virgin olive oil
10 sun-dried tomatoes, thinly sliced
30ml/2 tbsp capers, in brine or salted
115g/4oz/1 cup stoned black olives
2 garlic cloves, finely chopped
45ml/3 tbsp balsamic vinegar
45ml/3 tbsp chopped fresh parsley
salt and ground black pepper

1 Cook the pasta in plenty of boiling salted water until *al dente*. Drain and rinse under cold water to stop the cooking. Drain well and turn into a large bowl. Toss with the olive oil and set aside until required.

2 Soak the tomatoes in a bowl of hot water for 10 minutes. Do not discard the water. Rinse the capers well. If they have been preserved in salt, soak them in a little hot water for 10 minutes. Rinse again.

3 Combine the olives, tomatoes, capers, garlic and vinegar in a small bowl. Season with salt and ground black pepper.

4 Stir the olive mixture into the cooked pasta and toss well. Add 30–45ml/2–3 tbsp of the tomato soaking water if the salad seems too dry. Toss with the parsley and allow to stand for 15 minutes before serving.

Pasta, Melon and Prawn Salad

Orange cantaloupe or Charentais melon look spectacular in this salad. Or try a mixture of ogen, cantaloupe and water melon.

INGREDIENTS

Serves 4–6

175g/6oz pasta shapes

225g/8oz/2 cups frozen prawns, thawed and drained

1 large or 2 small melons

60ml/4 tbsp olive oil

15ml/1 tbsp tarragon vinegar

30ml/2 tbsp snipped fresh chives or chopped parsley

herb sprigs, to garnish

shredded Chinese leaves, to serve

1 Cook the pasta in boiling salted water according to the instructions on the packet. Drain well and allow to cool.

2 Peel the prawns and discard the shells.

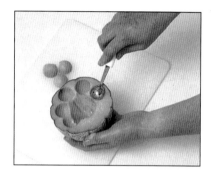

3 Halve the melon and remove the seeds with a teaspoon. Carefully scoop the flesh into balls with a melon baller and mix with the prawns and pasta.

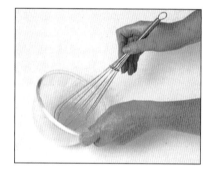

4 Whisk the oil, vinegar and chopped herbs together. Pour on to the prawn mixture and turn to coat. Cover and chill for at least 30 minutes.

5 Meanwhile shred the Chinese leaves and use to line a shallow bowl or the empty melon halves.

6 Pile the prawn mixture on to the Chinese leaves and garnish with sprigs of herbs.

Roquefort and Walnut Pasta Salad

This is a simple earthy salad, relying totally on the quality of the ingredients. There is no real substitute for Roquefort – a blue-veined ewe's-milk cheese which comes from south-western France.

INGREDIENTS

Serves 4

225g/8oz pasta shapes

mixed salad leaves, such as rocket, curly
    endive, lamb's lettuce, baby spinach,
    radicchio, etc

30ml/2 tbsp walnut oil

60ml/4 tbsp sunflower oil

30ml/2 tbsp red wine vinegar or
    sherry vinegar

225g/8oz Roquefort cheese,
    roughly crumbled

115g/4oz/1 cup walnut halves

salt and ground black pepper

1 Cook the pasta in plenty of boiling salted water according to the instructions on the packet. Drain well and cool. Wash and dry the salad leaves and place them in a large bowl.

2 Whisk together the walnut oil, sunflower oil, vinegar and salt and pepper to taste.

3 Pile the pasta in the centre of the leaves, scatter over the crumbled Roquefort and pour over the dressing.

4 Scatter over the walnuts. Toss just before serving.

COOK'S TIP

Try toasting the walnuts under the grill for a couple of minutes to release the flavour.

Wholemeal Pasta Salad

This substantial vegetarian salad is easily assembled from any combination of seasonal vegetables. Use raw or lightly blanched vegetables, or a mixture of both.

INGREDIENTS

Serves 8

450g/1lb short wholemeal pasta, such as
　fusilli or penne
45ml/3 tbsp olive oil
2 carrots
1 small bunch broccoli
175g/6oz/1½ cups shelled peas, fresh
　or frozen
1 red or yellow pepper
2 celery sticks
4 spring onions
1 large tomato
75g/3oz/¾ cup stoned olives
115g/4oz/1 cup diced Cheddar or
　mozzarella cheese or a combination
　of both
salt and ground black pepper

For the dressing
45ml/3 tbsp white wine or
　balsamic vinegar
60ml/4 tbsp olive oil
15ml/1 tbsp Dijon mustard
15ml/1 tbsp sesame seeds
10ml/2 tsp chopped mixed fresh herbs,
　such as parsley, thyme and basil

1 Cook the pasta in plenty of boiling salted water until *al dente*. Drain, and rinse under cold water to stop the cooking. Drain well and turn into a large bowl. Toss with 45ml/3 tbsp of the olive oil and set aside. Allow the pasta to cool completely.

2 Lightly blanch the carrots, broccoli and peas in a large pan of boiling water. Refresh under cold water. Drain well.

3 Chop the carrots and broccoli into bite-size pieces and add to the pasta with the peas. Slice the pepper, celery, spring onions and tomato into small pieces. Add them to the salad with the olives.

4 Make the dressing in a small bowl by combining the vinegar with the oil and mustard. Stir in the sesame seeds and herbs. Mix the dressing into the salad. Taste for seasoning, adding salt, pepper or more olive oil and vinegar if necessary. Stir in the cheese, then allow the salad to stand for about 15 minutes before serving.

Smoked Trout Pasta Salad

Bulb fennel gives this salad a lovely aniseed flavour.

Serves 6

15ml/1 tbsp butter

115g/4oz minced bulb fennel

6 spring onions, 2 minced and
    4 thinly sliced

225g/8oz skinless smoked trout
    fillets, flaked

45ml/3 tbsp chopped fresh dill

115g/4oz/½ cup mayonnaise

10ml/2 tsp fresh lemon juice

30ml/2 tbsp whipping cream

450g/1lb small pasta shapes, such as shells

salt and ground black pepper

fresh dill sprigs, to garnish

2 Add the sliced spring onions, trout, dill, mayonnaise, lemon juice and cream. Mix gently until well blended.

3 Cook the pasta in plenty of boiling salted water according to the instructions on the packet until *al dente*. Drain thoroughly and leave to cool.

4 Add the pasta to the vegetable and trout mixture and toss to coat evenly. Taste for seasoning and adjust if necessary. Serve the salad lightly chilled or at room temperature, garnished with dill.

1 Melt the butter in a small non-stick frying pan. Add the fennel and minced spring onions and season lightly with salt and black pepper. Cook over a medium heat for 3–5 minutes, or until just softened. Transfer to a large bowl and leave to cool slightly.

Artichoke Pasta Salad

Broccoli and black olives add colour to this delicious salad.

INGREDIENTS

Serves 4

105ml/7 tbsp olive oil

1 red pepper, quartered, seeded, and thinly sliced

1 onion, halved and thinly sliced

5ml/1 tsp dried thyme

45ml/3 tbsp sherry vinegar

450g/1lb pasta shapes, such as penne or fusilli

2 x 175g/6oz jars marinated artichoke hearts, drained and thinly sliced

150g/5oz cooked broccoli, chopped

20–25 salt-cured black olives, stoned and chopped

30ml/2 tbsp chopped fresh parsley

salt and ground black pepper

1 Heat 30ml/2 tbsp of the olive oil in a non-stick frying pan. Add the red pepper and onion and cook over a low heat until just soft, about 8–10 minutes, stirring from time to time.

2 Stir in the thyme, 1.5ml/¼ tsp salt and the vinegar. Cook, stirring, for a further 30 seconds, then set aside.

3 Cook the pasta in plenty of boiling salted water according to the instructions on the packet until *al dente*. Drain, rinse with hot water, then drain again. Transfer to a large bowl. Add 30ml/2 tbsp of the oil and toss well to coat thoroughly.

4 Add the artichokes, broccoli, olives, parsley, onion mixture and remaining oil to the pasta. Season with salt and pepper. Stir to blend. Leave to stand for at least 1 hour before serving or chill overnight. Serve the salad at room temperature.

Pasta and Beetroot Salad

Colour is vital at a party table, and this salad is certainly eye-catching. Prepare the egg and avocado at the last moment to avoid discoloration.

Serves 8

2 uncooked beetroots, scrubbed

225g/8oz pasta shells or twists

45ml/3 tbsp vinaigrette dressing

2 celery sticks, thinly sliced

3 spring onions, sliced

75g/3oz/¾ cup walnuts or hazelnuts, roughly chopped

1 eating apple, cored, halved and sliced

salt and ground black pepper

For the dressing

60ml/4 tbsp mayonnaise

45ml/3 tbsp natural yogurt or fromage frais

30ml/2 tbsp milk

10ml/2 tsp creamed horseradish

To serve

curly lettuce leaves

3 eggs, hard-boiled and chopped

2 ripe avocados

1 box salad cress

1 Boil the beetroots, without peeling, in lightly salted water until they are just tender, about 1 hour. Drain, cool, then peel and chop. Set aside.

2 Cook the pasta in plenty of boiled salted water according to the instructions on the packet. Drain, toss in the vinaigrette and season well. Leave to cool then mix with the beetroot, celery, onions, nuts and apple in a bowl.

3 Stir all the dressing ingredients together and then mix into the pasta. Chill well.

4 To serve, line a salad bowl with the lettuce and spoon in the salad. Scatter over the chopped egg. Peel and slice the avocados and arrange them on top then sprinkle over the cress.

Tuna Pasta Salad

*This easy pasta salad uses canned
beans and tuna for a quick main
course dish.*

INGREDIENTS

Serves 6–8

450g/1lb short pasta, such as macaroni or
    farfalle

60ml/4 tbsp olive oil

2 x 200g/7oz cans tuna, drained
    and flaked

2 x 400g/14oz cans cannellini or borlotti
    beans, rinsed and drained

1 small red onion

2 celery sticks

juice of 1 lemon

30ml/2 tbsp chopped fresh parsley

salt and ground black pepper

1 Cook the pasta in plenty of
boiling salted water until a*l
dente.* Drain, and rinse under cold
water to stop the cooking. Drain
well and turn into a large bowl.
Toss with the olive oil and set
aside. Allow to cool completely.

2 Mix the flaked tuna and the
beans into the cooked pasta.
Slice the onion and celery very
thinly and add them to the pasta.

3 Combine the lemon juice with
the parsley. Mix into the other
ingredients. Season with salt and
pepper. Allow the salad to stand
for at least 1 hour before serving.

Chicken Pasta Salad

*This salad uses leftover chicken from
a roast or a cold poached chicken
breast if you prefer.*

INGREDIENTS

Serves 4

350g/12oz short pasta, such as mezze,
    rigatoni, fusilli or penne

45ml/3 tbsp olive oil

225g/8oz cold cooked chicken

2 small red and yellow peppers

50g/2oz/½ cup stoned green olives

4 spring onions, chopped

45ml/3 tbsp mayonnaise

5ml/1 tsp Worcestershire sauce

15ml/1 tbsp white wine vinegar

salt and ground black pepper

a few fresh basil leaves, to garnish

1 Cook the pasta in plenty of
boiling salted water until *al
dente.* Drain, and rinse under cold
water to stop the cooking. Drain
well and turn into a large bowl.
Toss with the olive oil and set
aside. Allow to cool completely.

2 Cut the chicken into bite-size
pieces, removing any bones.
Cut the peppers into small pieces.

3 Combine all the ingredients
except the pasta in a medium
bowl. Taste for seasoning, then mix
into the pasta. Serve well chilled,
garnished with basil leaves.

DESSERTS

~

Strawberry Conchiglie Salad

A divinely decadent dessert laced with cherry liqueur and luscious raspberry sauce.

INGREDIENTS

Serves 4

175g/6oz dried conchiglie

225g/8oz raspberries, thawed if frozen

15–30ml/1–2 tbsp caster sugar

lemon juice

450g/1lb small fresh strawberries

flaked almonds

45ml/3 tbsp kirsch

salt

1 Cook the pasta in a large saucepan of lightly salted, boiling water for 8–10 minutes, until tender, but still firm to the bite. Drain well and set aside to cool completely.

2 Purée the raspberries in a food processor and rub through a strainer. Put the purée and sugar in a small saucepan and simmer, stirring occasionally, for 5–6 minutes. Stir in lemon juice to taste and set aside to cool.

3 Hull the strawberries and cut in half if large. Toss with the pasta and transfer to a serving bowl.

4 Spread out the almonds on a baking sheet and toast under the grill until golden, then cool.

5 Stir the kirsch into the raspberry sauce and pour it over the salad. Scatter the toasted almonds on top and serve.

Dark Chocolate Ravioli

This is a spectacular chocolate pasta, with cocoa powder added to the flour. The pasta packets contain a sumptuous white chocolate and cream cheese filling.

Serves 4

175g/6oz plain white flour

25g/1oz cocoa powder

30ml/2 tbsp icing sugar

2 large eggs

single cream and grated chocolate,
    to serve

For the filling

175g/6oz white chocolate

350g/12oz cream cheese

2 eggs

1 Make the pasta dough following the instructions in the Introduction, but sift the flour with the cocoa powder and icing sugar before adding the eggs. Cover and set aside to rest for at least 30 minutes.

2 For the filling, break up the white chocolate and melt it in a basin standing over a pan of barely simmering water. Cool slightly, then beat in the cream cheese and 1 egg. Spoon into a piping bag fitted with a plain nozzle.

3 Cut the pasta dough in half and wrap one portion in clear film. Roll the dough out thinly to a rectangle on a lightly floured surface, or use a pasta machine to roll out thinly. Cover with a clean, damp tea towel and repeat with the remaining pasta dough.

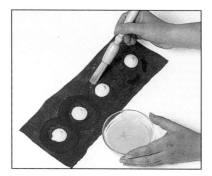

4 Pipe small mounds of the chocolate and cream cheese filling in even rows, spacing them at 4cm/1½in intervals, across one piece of the dough. Beat the remaining egg and lightly brush the spaces of dough between the mounds with it.

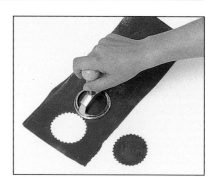

5 Using a rolling pin, lift the remaining sheet of pasta over the dough with the filling. Press down firmly between the pockets of filling, pushing out any trapped air. Cut into rounds with a serrated ravioli cutter or a sharp knife. Transfer to a floured tea towel and set aside to rest for 1 hour.

6 Bring a large pan of lightly salted water to the boil and add the ravioli, a few at a time, stirring to prevent them from sticking together. Simmer gently for about 3–5 minutes, remove with a slotted spoon and serve with single cream and grated chocolate.

Apple and Rhubarb Noodle Pudding

This is delicious hot or cold. The richness is offset by the tart flavours of apple and rhubarb.

INGREDIENTS

Serves 4–6

50g/2oz dried short-cut macaroni

50g/2oz butter

30ml/2 tbsp light brown sugar

2 cooking apples, peeled, cored and cut into eighths

225g/8oz rhubarb, cut into 2.5cm/ 1in lengths

pinch of ground cinnamon

115g/4oz cream cheese

75g/3oz caster sugar

2 eggs

250ml/8fl oz/1 cup whipping cream

few drops of vanilla essence

pinch of grated nutmeg

icing sugar, for dusting

1 Preheat the oven to 180°C/ 350°F/Gas 4. Grease one or two ovenproof dishes with a little butter. Melt the remaining butter in a frying pan, add the brown sugar and stir until it dissolves. Add the apples and rhubarb, stirring to coat. Sprinkle the cinnamon into the pan and cook for 3–5 minutes.

2 Meanwhile, cook the macaroni in a saucepan of boiling water for 8–10 minutes, until tender, but still firm to the bite. Drain, rinse under cold water and drain again.

3 In a bowl, beat the cream cheese, caster sugar and eggs together until smooth. Stir in the cream and vanilla and mix well. Fold in the macaroni and the fruit mixture, then spoon the mixture into the prepared dishes.

4 Sprinkle the nutmeg over the top. Set the dishes in a roasting tin, then pour hot water into the tin to the depth of 2.5cm/1in. Bake for about 35 minutes, until set. Dust with icing sugar and serve hot or cold.

Pasta Timbales with Apricot Sauce

Orzo or rice-shaped pasta inspired this dessert made like a rice pudding, but with a difference! Other small soup pasta can be used if orzo cannot be found.

INGREDIENTS

Serves 4

115g/4oz dried orzo or other
    soup pasta

75g/3oz caster sugar

25g/1oz butter

1 vanilla pod, split

750ml/1¼ pints/3⅔ cups milk

300ml/½ pint/1¼ cups ready-
    made custard

45ml/3 tbsp kirsch

15m/1 tbsp powdered gelatine

oil, for greasing

400g/14oz can apricots in juice

lemon juice

salt

fresh flowers, to decorate (optional)

1 Place the orzo or other pasta, the sugar, a pinch of salt, the butter, vanilla pod and milk in a heavy-based saucepan and bring to the boil. Lower the heat and simmer, stirring frequently, for about 25 minutes until the pasta is tender and most of the liquid has been absorbed.

2 Remove and discard the vanilla pod and transfer the pasta to a bowl to cool completely. Then stir in the custard and 30ml/2 tbsp of the kirsch.

3 Sprinkle the gelatine over 45ml/3 tbsp water in a small bowl. Set the bowl in a pan of barely simmering water. Allow to become spongy and heat gently to dissolve. Stir it into the pasta in a thin continuous stream.

4 Lightly oil 4 timbale moulds and spoon in the pasta. Refrigerate for 2 hours, until set.

5 Meanwhile, purée the apricots in a food processor and rub through a strainer. Stir in lemon juice to taste and the remaining kirsch.

6 Loosen the timbales from their moulds and turn out on to plates. Spoon some apricot sauce around them and serve, decorated with fresh flowers, if liked.

Index